THE MOST INSPIRA
FOR YO

15
AMAZING & INSPIRING
TRUE TALES

FROM MODERN SOCCER GREATS

TERRENCE ARMSTRONG

CONTENTS

Introduction 1

Lionel Messi: The Smallest Player on the Field 3

Kylian Mbappé: Overcoming Poverty.............................11

Asa Hartford: Playing with a Hole in Your Heart................19

Neymar: The Power of Self-Belief 27

Jude Bellingham: You Don't Need to Love Soccer Immediately!........35

Kaka: Playing After a Spinal Injury 43

Christiano Ronaldo: Poverty and Heart Disease................51

Mohamed Salah: Village Kid Turned Global Superstar.........................59

Antoine Griezmann: Overcoming Failure 67

Luka Modric: Living As a Refugee.................................77

Karim Benzema: Leaving Ganglife Behind 85

Kevin de Bruyne: Surviving Teenage Angst 93

Vinicius Junior: From The Streets To Conquering The World 101

Zinedine Zidane: Legendary Player & Coach....................109

Sam Kerr: Playing In A Male Dominated Sport 117

Bonus Material: Inspirational soccer stories.....................125

INTRODUCTION

Soccer has been played for hundreds of years in one form or another. After all, at its core, it is essentially just kicking a ball around.

The first organized soccer game was held in December of 1863. That game was the genesis of what we know as soccer today.

Over the years, there have been many great soccer players. Some have natural talent, while others have overcome huge issues both in their personal lives and on the field to become great.

Their actions on and off the field should inspire and motivate you to be more like them. You don't have to be a great soccer player to learn their lessons and apply them to your own life!

Let's take a look at 15 of the most amazing modern soccer players.

LIONEL MESSI
THE SMALLEST PLAYER ON
THE FIELD

Lionel Messi is one of the greatest soccer players in the world. He's the smallest player on the field, something that stems from a growth disorder when he was a child.

He was fortunate because his parents fought tooth and nail to get him the treatment he needed, allowing him to eventually reach 5ft 6in. Without their dedication, the world wouldn't have the Messi that we all know and love.

But his parent's struggle (and ultimate triumph) also taught Messi a valuable lesson—one that he has used time and time again on the field.

Messi may be one of the best soccer players alive today, but that doesn't mean he hasn't had his ups and downs!

Commonly known as Leo, Lionel Messi played his first professional soccer game for Barcelona at the tender age of 16. His first League game followed when he was 17. Now, over 20 years later, he's the all-time top scorer for both Argentina and Barcelona.

His list of achievements is impressive!

Messi's first League game was for Barcelona when he was just 17. He was wearing the number 30 when the team played

Albacete in May of 2005. His arrival and participation were eagerly anticipated, and Messi didn't disappoint.

As the game started, Messi was kept in reserve. Barcelona played well, gaining a 1-0 advantage. This allowed the coach to replace Samuel Eto'o with Messi, 87 minutes into the game.

Just two minutes after Messi stepped onto the field, Ronaldinho passed him the ball, setting Messi up for a shot and his first goal. Unfortunately, it was ruled as offside.

Scoring a goal in the first two minutes of your debut play is something special, even if it was ruled out. But Messi went one step further! Two minutes later, at 91 minutes into the game, Ronaldinho passed to Messi again. Messi lobbed the ball over the keeper's head and into the back of the net, scoring the first of many goals.

In August of 2005, Messi didn't fare quite as well, as he made his international debut in a friendly match against Argentina. Messi waited until the 63rd minute to start playing, but just two minutes after getting on the field, he was sent off with a red card. The referee said Messi had elbowed Argentina defender Vilmos Vanczak. Messi denied it.

Fortunately, this rocky start helped him focus on keeping his play clean.

Messi's impressive play with Barcelona led to him being included in the Argentinian World Cup squad in 2006. He was substituted onto the field in the 74th minute. The team was already ahead, but Messi still made his mark. He scored the sixth goal for Argentina, sealing their victory 6-0 and becoming the youngest player to score at the World Cup.

Messi's triumphs on the field continued, and by 2007 he had become a household name. This was the year Barcelona played

Real Madrid and Messi scored three goals in one match. The hat trick was even more impressive considering how good the Real Madrid players were.

One of Messi's best goals ever also came in 2007. In April of that year, he dribbled his way through a sea of Getafe defenders, setting himself up for a shot that he simply powered home.

2007 was definitely the year Messi became known as one of the greatest soccer players on the planet.

2009 was another good year for Messi. He'd been in the Champions League since 2006, but by 2009 he was an established and recognizable force. By the end of his 2009 campaign, he was the tournament's top scorer. He also scored in the final against Manchester United, ensuring Barcelona took the crown.

Of course, even the greatest player in the world has agonizing moments. Messi was part of the 2010 Argentinian World Cup squad. Hopes were high and the pressure was really on. Unfortunately, Messi struggled with that pressure. Argentina bowed out in the quarterfinals, beaten by Germany 4-0! The legendary Maradona coached the Argentinian team and was fired for his failure to lift the World Cup. At the same time, Messi was accused of caring more for his club than his country.

It was a low moment for Messi, but only the first of his World Cup defeats.

In 2014, Messi showed the Argentinian fans that his passion was as great for his country as it was for his club. He took the Golden Ball Award as the player of the tournament. However, despite his skill, Argentina still struggled in the last game, losing 1-0 to Germany.

At the club level, Messi was busy breaking every record and scoring more goals than any other player. However, in 2016, he also became the leading goal scorer of all time for Argentina. Unfortunately, Argentina still lost the Copa America final, finishing second to Chile.

Dejected, Messi decided he had reached his peak. His track record at the international level didn't match his club records, and he announced he was retiring from international soccer.

Fortunately, the fans knew better. They campaigned, along with Argentinian president Mauricio Macri, and convinced Messi that he had more to give. He continued playing internationally, with the simple mantra "My love for my country and this shirt is too great."

Messi didn't see an instant turnaround in his fortunes. The 2018 World Cup campaign was the worst Argentina had seen in years. Then, the Copa America of 2019 saw Argentina relegated to third place. Messi was sent off in the 37th minute and refused to accept the third-place trophy, stating that his sending-off was a result of his criticism of the fielders and referees.

The result was a three-month international ban.

By 2020, things were starting to look really bad for Messi. Barcelona lost in the Champions League quarterfinals to Bayern Munich, something that could only be described as embarrassing. This, along with disagreements with team management, spelt the end of his 20+ years with Barcelona.

In 2021, he joined Paris Saint-Germain. This was the start of a new era that included the 2022 World Cup, where Messi finally led Argentina to victory. He scored two goals in the 3-3 draw, as well as the first of the penalties, cementing his place as the greatest player of all time.

FUN FACTS ABOUT LIONEL MESSI

- Leo has won the Ballon d'Or seven times—more than anyone else.
- He scored 91 goals in 2012, setting the record!
- His first League goal was on May 1, 2005, when he was just 17 years old.
- Leo first wore the number 19 for Barcelona. He got the number 10 when his mentor and idol Ronaldinho left in 2008.
- Every time he scores, he looks up and points to the sky in recognition of his grandmother.
- At just 24, he became the top scorer of all time for Barcelona!
- Messi temporarily retired after missing a penalty at the 2016 World Cup and sending Argentina home.
- He created the Leo Messi Foundation, which helps vulnerable children get the education and health care they need.

QUICK TRIVIA TEST

How old was Messi when he first played for Barcelona?

16.

When did Messi win his first Ballon d'Or?

In 2009—he was 22.

How many Ballon d'Or's has Messi won?

Seven.

What year did Messi finally lead Argentina to World Cup victory?

2022.

Why did Messi leave Barcelona?

Disagreements with management.

FIVE LIFE LESSONS

1. Never quit!

Messi is one of the greatest soccer stars of all time, yet he didn't win a World Cup until 2022. This shows that, no matter what your goal, you can make it if you don't quit.

2. Go with your instinct.

This isn't just true on the field. In most situations in life, you should trust your gut, since you normally know what needs to be done. As Messi put it, "The best decisions aren't made with your mind but with your instinct."

3. Be consistent.

It's rare to get what you want straight away. If you have dreams, then you're going to need to fight to make them come true. The simplest approach is to consistently operate at the highest standard.

4. Size doesn't matter.

Messi has always been the smallest man on the field, yet he is also the most talented. The truth is, you don't need to be big or small to chase your dream and achieve your goals. Size really doesn't matter—it's all about your determination.

5. You can't always win.

Messi is arguably one of the greatest soccer players to ever have lived, but even he doesn't win every game he plays.

That's true in every area of life. in order to win the battle or achieve your dream, you have to be prepared to lose on the way there.

KYLIAN MBAPPÈ
OVERCOMING POVERTY

Kylian Mbappé was born in Paris in 1998. Although his family eventually moved, they stayed in the vicinity of Paris, allowing him to grow up near some of the best soccer clubs in France.

While he was young, Mbappé was sent to a local private Catholic school. The teachers believed he was highly intelligent, but that his unruly behavior kept him from excelling. That said, he applied himself when he wanted to. Mbappé started learning Spanish at 15, and is now fluent!

Mbappé's dad was a soccer coach, and he had the pleasure of coaching his song for the first time when he was just six years old. Prior to that, Mbappé had a genuine interest in the game, but his dad didn't appreciate his skill level.

The moment he coached his son for the first time, Mbappé 's father knew he was special. His dribbling skills and speed were already better than children older than him. His father coached him for several years, teaching him everything he could about the beautiful game. Then, when he turned 11, Real Madrid invited Mbappé to train with their under-12 squad.

For Mbappé, it was a dream come true. A chance to become an international soccer player like his idol Zinedine Zidane.

But he also had offers coming in from other clubs. By the age of 14, he had shown the world his skills while playing for the Chelsea youth team against Charlton Athletic.

When it came time to sign the 14-year-old prodigy, it was the youth academy in Monaco that made the best offer. Mbappé signed with them for three years.

Two years into the contract, he was brought onto the Monaco reserve team. Thanks to Mbappé's skill, he was added to the main squad just three weeks later.

At the beginning of December 2015, Mbappé came on to play against Caen. He was substituted onto the field after 88 minutes, making him the youngest-ever player at Monaco.

This was the start of a momentous journey.

Mbappé's first goal came a couple of months later, in February 2016, while Monaco was playing Troyes. His goal in stoppage time cemented Monaco's win and made him the youngest goal-scorer in Monaco's history.

He was just getting started!

In December 2016, when Monaco was playing Rennes, Mbappé impressively scored his first hat trick, helping Monaco win 7-0!

Just two months later, he scored another hat trick, this time against Metz. It was his first official League hat trick, but there were plenty more to come.

2017 was an excellent year for Mbappé. Although still new to the League, he was eager to showcase his talents. He started in March by scoring Monaco's opening goal in the second leg of the Champions League. His success at scoring away goals helped Monaco move through to the quarterfinals. Sadly, the team was eliminated in the semifinals.

However, Mbappé had made his mark. It was also the year he scored his 25th Champions League goal. In fact, he was credited with 26 goals in 44 matches and was instrumental in helping Monaco win the League title.

Mbappé himself remained calm, even during the most stressful games. This was a skill he learned from his teammate, Radamel Falcao, and one that has served him well.

Unsurprisingly, Mbappé was in demand. Following a heartfelt speech by Unai Emery at Mbappé's home, he agreed to transfer to Paris Saint Germain (PSG). He was signed over on loan from Monaco with a mandatory purchase option of $180 million. That made Mbappé the second most expensive player in the world, ever. Only Neymar went for more!

Mbappé's debut with PSG went well. He scored one goal and helped the team secure a 5-1 victory. This was followed by a goal against Celtic—Mbappé's first European goal.

However, it was his help setting up Neymar for a goal against Bayern Munich that really showed his abilities to the world. A clever feint against a defender that involved the ball rolling under his foot allowed him to move past and give Neymar a perfect shot.

That one move told the world that Mbappé was worth the transfer fee.

In recognition of his skill, PSG gave him the number 7 shirt for the 2018-2019 season. This was a number that had been proudly worn by some of the best PSG players ever.

Mbappé lived up to the hype. The first game of the season saw him score twice inside the last 10 minutes! His speed and ball control simply couldn't be matched. As the season progressed, Mbappé managed to score in every match. Eventually, PSG played against Nimes. Although Mbappé did score in this game, it was also the first time he was sent off with a red card.

The referee ruled that Mbappe had shoved Teji Savanier after Savanier had completed a late challenge from behind. Despite being sent off, Mbappé was unrepentant, stating that he would do it again because he couldn't tolerate this blatant disregarding of the rules.

Mbappé officially joined PSG in the 2018-2019 season, after being on loan for 2017-2018. During his time at PSG, he scored 166 League goals from 192 appearances. That's a record that may never be beaten!

Mbappé has set the soccer world alight in the first 25 years of his life, and he's not done yet. This is reflected in some of his greatest moments on the field.

In 2019, Mbappé scored a goal against Nantes with a back-heel, after receiving an outside-of-the-foot pass. Fans and fellow players alike were blown away!

His skill has also carried PSG to victory on more than one occasion. For example, when PSG was struggling against Saint Etienne in February 2019, Mbappé dug deep, turning a chipped ball into a volley straight into the goal. It won PSG the game.

Of course, one of the highlights of his career has been the 2018 World Cup. During the tournament, Mbappé scored four goals and assisted with many others. In the final of the World Cup, he shot from outside the box and scored. It wasn't his best-looking goal, but it did make him the youngest player to score in a World Cup final since the legend Pele.

Naturally, his best goals are those where he makes a play from nothing. For example, when PSG was playing Lyon in the French Cup. Mbappé was by himself, with several defenders and a goalie in front of him. He showed stunning ball control by getting around the defenders and sliding the ball into the net, past the helpless keeper.

The goals that motivate his team the most are those that result from a team effort. That's what happened when PSG faced off against Barcelona in the Champions League 2021.

PSG was down one goal, but Mbappé's skill and determination saw him drive home an unstoppable equalizer after the rest of the team had moved the ball perfectly around the field. They went on to win 4-1, with Mbappé scoring three of those goals.

Another milestone was reached by Mbappé in 2021 when he scored two goals for PSG against Lyon, helping them to a 4-2 victory and securing him 100 goals for PSG in his short career.

Mbappé has been rumored to be facing personal problems, but he doesn't bring them onto the field. Instead, he allows his ball-control skills to do the talking. There's little doubt he's got a lot more to give and a lot more records to break, proving anything is possible.

FUN FACTS ABOUT MBAPPÈ

- Mbappé was the second teenager to ever score a goal in a World Cup final. Pelé was the first.
- He was the cover star of EA Sports' "FIFA 21."
- Mbappé has over 100 pairs of shoes!
- He's the global ambassador for Hublot, the Swiss watchmaker.
- He's the only player to have scored four goals against Barcelona in one match.

QUICK TRIVIA TEST

How old was Mbappé when he scored in the World Cup final?

19.

Who was Mbappé's first idol?

Zinedine Zidane

When did Mbappé make his first team debut?

December 2015.

Who does Mbappé have a sponsorship deal with?

Hublot.

At what age did he score his 25th Champions League goal?

19.

FIVE LIFE LESSONS

1. Perseverance matters.

Mbappé is naturally talented, but that doesn't mean his rise to stardom was easy. He persevered through all obstacles to reach the top. That's a lesson everyone should learn—success is only possible if you persevere.

2. Set goals.

Another key to success is setting goals. Pick a goal you want to achieve, envision it in your head, and then work toward it every day. That's what Mbappé does!

3. Keep your feet on the ground.

Successful soccer players earn a lot of money and can have almost anything they want. It's easy to start believing the world should revolve around you. But Mbappé is still humble and credits this to the strong influences around him. You need to do the same and remain grounded, no matter how successful you are. This will help to keep things in perspective.

4. Give back when you can.

Mbappé, along with many other major celebrities, likes to give back. It's easier now than ever before because he can share through social media, create foundations, and give to good causes.

Whether you're successful or not, you should always look for ways to give back and help others.

5. Make every opportunity count.

You never know when you're going to get an opportunity, so if you're offered one, make the most of it. Who knows where it could lead!

Take a look at Mbappé's 2016-2017 season. On the European stage, he scored 15 goals and assisted with 11 others. Yet, he didn't start in any of those games!

ASA HARTFORD PLAYING WITH A HOLE IN YOUR HEART

Asa Hartford is retired now, but he's proof that, if your desire is strong enough, you can play soccer regardless of what obstacles are placed in your path.

His love of soccer began at a very young age. Fortunately, his skills were good enough to let him become professional. Hartford started playing for Drumchapel Amateurs and was soon spotted by West Bromwich Albion. They offered him a spot on the first team, and his professional career started well, he was just 17 at the time. He helped the team to the FA Cup Final and the League final.

Naturally, his talents were spotted by other teams. He was eventually invited to transfer to Leeds United. However, a standard medical was performed before the transfer, and it was discovered that he had a hole in his heart.

At the time, Leeds was struggling. Many of their players were injured and the team was struggling to compete in Division One.

Hartford was an obvious choice. He was clearly talented. In fact, the success of West Bromwich Albion was directly attributable to him. Leeds had already tried to get Hartford twice, with Bromwich saying no.

This time, they said yes, and a deal was struck. But then Hartford failed his medical. That was when he found out he had a hole in his heart. It was a slight defect, one that he had been born with, and had never affected his ability to play competitive soccer.

But in an instant, just hours before he was due to play his first game for Leeds, Hartford had his dream destroyed.

West Bromwich was happy to keep Hartford. He had passed his medical with them and was seen as one of the fittest players on the team. West Bromwich even referred him to a specialist, who stated that the hole in his heart shouldn't cause any issues for his career.

The specialist confirmed no surgery was necessary, and Hartford was back with the team, training within a week.

Unfortunately, the debacle took its toll. Leeds fans were shocked and spent the entire season thinking about what could have been, especially when they finished as runners-up in their league.

It also took its toll on Hartford. His first match after the medical diagnosis was against Nottingham Forest. West Brom lost 4-1. This was partly due to the team feeling the pressure and being too disorganized. But it was also a result of Hartford's news. For the first half of the game, he no longer looked like a rising star. Every move he made was the safe option—protecting himself, pacing himself, and avoiding confrontations.

Fortunately, he seemed to snap out of it in the second half and set up a variety of plays. Sadly, his teammates couldn't finish the job.

Hartford was lucky. By the end of the match, he had reconciled the issue and was firmly focused on the future. He may have wished he was playing for Leeds, but he was committed to playing well, no matter where he was.

Fortunately for Hartford, that's not where his story ends.

There's little doubt that the next three years were tough for Hartford. He continued to play at West Bromwich and he continued to excel in midfield. However, there were clues that the Leeds transfer debacle had affected him. Simple mistakes added up, and Hartford struggled to fully commit and regain his form.

It's not surprising that the medical issue sent everyone around him into a panicked state. Everyone involved felt that his life was at risk, and that playing would make it worse. With everyone around him believing this, it was hard for him not to be concerned. That's likely the reason that Hartford's play was affected.

Of course, being called up to Scotland's national team less than a year after the Leeds affair helped to restore his confidence. He ended up playing in two World Cup tournaments for Scotland.

Then, he was suddenly offered a transfer to Manchester City, another dream offer that Hartford probably hadn't expected. He had spent 7 years at Bromwich and probably thought that was where he was destined to stay.

Manchester already knew about the hole in his heart, but they weren't worried. Shortly after signing, Hartford was put on the field and his talent was magically restored.

The simple restoration of confidence in his abilities transformed his game. Suddenly, Hartford wasn't making simple mistakes. He was a valuable asset to the team, instrumental in propelling them to win the League.

With renewed confidence and improved play, Hartford was approached by Nottingham Forest. They spent $500,000 transferring him to their team, another dream of his.

It was a bumpy ride for the soccer superstar. Nottingham Forest didn't go well. The events obviously took a toll on Hartford, his confidence had taken a knock and his play on the field suffered.

But not for long, after Nottingham came a period with Everton. Then, he went back to Maine Road. His form returned and ultimately transferred to Fort Lauderdale in Florida, where he was their star player.

There is little doubt that Hartford was an extremely talented midfielder. When he eventually retired from the game he moved into management. His expertise has been invaluable, proving there is more to this legend than just being awesome on the field.

FUN FACTS ABOUT ASA HARTFORD

- Hartford was named after his father's favorite singer, Asa Jolson.
- After a lot of hype, his move to Nottingham Forest lasted only a few weeks.
- He picked up his first League Cup winners medal in 1976!
- In his second professional game, Hartford played against Bobby Charlton and George Best—and he scored a goal!
- West Bromwich signed him and his best friend, Hughie Reed, at the same time.

QUICK TRIVIA TEST

At what age did Asa Hartford make his professional debut?

In 1967 for West Bromwich—he was 17.

Which club canceled his transfer due to medical problems?

Leeds.

How long did Hartford play for West Bromwich Albion?

Seven years.

How many World Cups did Hartford play in?

Two.

What did Hartford do when he retired from professional soccer?

Soccer management.

FIVE LIFE LESSONS

1. Don't let anyone tell you something is impossible.

It would have been easy for Hartford to give up after being told he had a hole in his heart, especially as it cost him a transfer to Leeds.

He didn't give up, and neither should you. Hartford missed just one game with Bromwich thanks to his health scare, and it never caused him an issue on the field.

2. Don't be afraid to dream.

Hartford had a simple dream and plenty of talent. But, no matter how great his talent, it took hard work to make it as a professional soccer player, especially with his personal setbacks.

His dream was to be a professional soccer player, and he gave it his all and succeeded. You can, and should, follow your dream!

3. Be consistent.

Hartford is one of West Bromwich Albion's most beloved players. He achieved legendary status, and it was not just because he was potentially the best midfielder of his generation.

He also consistently gave his all to the team. The fans noticed and respected this. Being consistent will earn the respect of others.

4. Never stop challenging yourself.

Hartford could have stopped playing after he found out about the hole in his heart. Instead, he pushed himself and built a successful career as a professional soccer player.

After his retirement, he moved into coaching, consistently challenging himself to do more and be better. That is something everyone should try to do, every day.

5. Remember that what you do affects others.

If you look online, you will find many people who have fond memories of Hartford from when he played. Some were impressed with his skill; others appreciated his attitude and the way he conducted himself both on and off the field.

If you really want to make it big, you need to remember that what you do affects those around you—and it is those people who can impact your success or failure.

I have included these free downloadable gifts to help light up your inner inspiration & reach your potential.

While you are reading through the stories, lessons and trivia, we recommend that you make use of all the bonuses we've attached here!

All our bonuses have been made specifically to help young athletes feel fired up, get inspired from the best to ever do it, and most importantly fall more in love with this incredible game!

Here's a list of what you're getting:

1) 250 Fun Facts From The World Of Sports
2) Sports Practice and Game Calendar
3) 5 Fun Exercise Drills for Kids
4) The BEST Advice From The Greatest Athletes Of All Time
5) The Mental Mindset Guided Meditation & Affirmation Collection
6) The Most Famous Events In Sports History And What They Can Teach Us

Now, it's over to you to scan the QR code, follow the instructions & get started!

NEYMAR
THE POWER OF SELF-BELIEF

Neymar was born in Brazil in February 1992 and is today widely regarded as one of the best soccer players in the world.

Like many of the greats, Neymar comes from a poor background. But soccer was not his motivation to get away from his humble beginnings. He was simply a child with immense talent.

As a kid, he did what all the other children did—played soccer in the streets. He was first spotted playing with a ball on a beach in his hometown. He wasn't even playing proper soccer! But the coach, Betinho, saw how coordinated and agile Neymar was as he ran through the sand.

These skills are incredibly useful in the game of soccer.

With the help and guidance of his coach, his skills led him to play for Portuguesa Santista, followed by Santos. It was at Santos where he first played professionally, at the tender age of 17. That's when the world started to see the magic of Neymar! He only played the last 30 minutes of his first professional game, but in that time he displayed enough skill to get himself back on the field the following week. That's when he scored his first professional goal.

In his first season, he scored 14 goals out of 48 games. But that actually wasn't too surprising. After all, Neymar is an extremely talented player. What sets him apart is his ability to score seemingly impossible goals. He's also known for his ability to control the ball, mislead opponents, and delicately tap the ball into the back of the net.

His incredible skill once allowed him to fool three defenders and the goalkeeper in 2015 when Brazil played a friendly against the US. Lucas Moura passed Neymar the ball, and it came in at a diagonal. He positioned his body to shoot the ball at the far side of the net, but his delicate footwork allowed him to direct the ball to the near post and into the back of the net.

Neymar's biggest issue on the field has never been his skills or even a particularly good defender—it has been his teammates!

For most of his international career with Brazil, the team also included Ronaldinho—a player whom Neymar has often been compared to. Ronaldinho was already established as one of the greats, which meant Neymar was often considered a supporting act, despite scoring 79 goals for Brazil!

That's why he worked extra hard to score some truly fantastic goals. For example, when Brazil played Paraguay in 2017, Neymar was still in the middle of the Brazil half when he received the ball. With a number of players heading toward him, he set off at a blistering pace, dribbling the ball down the touchline and deftly past the first two attackers. This allowed him to move into the penalty area. Still moving at an incredible pace, he dribbled around another player and shot the ball toward the net. Three defenders were running straight at him, giving him no time and very little angle. Neymar chose to clip the shot, and despite a small deflection, it dropped into the back of the net, securing Brazil a place in the 2018 World Cup.

His run, from receiving the ball to shooting, was an astonishing 64 meters long. Of course, that has become a trademark Neymar move.

Neymar also played alongside Lionel Messi at Paris Saint Germain and Barcelona. While both players are talented, Messi had seniority and a better goal record. In other words, Neymar lived in Messi's shadow—a reality that was challenging for him.

Despite being overshadowed by some of the best players of all time, Neymar has a history of impressive goals. Perhaps one of his most memorable was back in 2011 when he won the FIFA Puskas Award for best goal. This was made even more impressive by the fact that he was still relatively new to professional soccer—plus, he beat Messi, who was also up for the award.

The goal was classic Neymar. He dribbled down the field, passing the ball back and forth with his teammate, then eventually exploding into action. It was the deft pass from his right foot to his left, and then back to the right, that threw off the defenders. That gave him the shot, which he clipped past the goalie.

Like any true hero, Neymar needed to experience a stumble to reach his true potential. Perhaps the most stunning miss of his career was in 2014. Brazil was playing Ecuador, the score was 0-0, and Neymar found himself in the box, perfectly lined up for the incoming cross.

He was just three yards from the goal, but somehow kicked the ball wrong. It hit the bar and bounced back toward him. It was moving too fast for him to control, and the goalkeeper wrapped his arms around it.

Experiences like these are great learning moments. Neymar recovered his composure and went on to deliver a stunning pass to Willian, allowing him to score and clinch the win for Brazil.

Continuing after such an easy miss can be difficult, but Neymar rose to the challenge and has continued to deliver stunning goals ever since. Of particular note was his goal in the World Cup game against Bolivia in 2023, which was part of the 2026 World Cup qualifiers.

Brazil won 5-1, with Neymar scoring two goals. Those were his 78th and 79th goals for Brazil, taking him past Pelé's record and beating Brazil's all-time goal-scoring record.

What was truly impressive about this performance was that Neymar had missed a penalty kick in the 17th minute. He has an 82.5% success rate for penalties, but he missed the goal. Still, he managed to recover his composure. Neymar's two goals were in the second half, in the 61st and 78th minutes, respectively. Both were from low crosses directly to him, allowing Neymar to display his trademark finish and traditional 'neener neener' face.

Neymar has already proved he is as inspirational as he is great— and there's still a lot more to come.

FUN FACTS ABOUT NEYMAR

- In 2013, Neymar transferred to Barcelona for €57.1 million.
- He was partnered with Messi and Suarez in Barcelona, and they became known as the most lethal attacking trio in soccer.
- His 2017 transfer to PSG had a €222 million fee, the largest ever.
- Neymar has his own comic book series!
- Neymar is also passionate about basketball.

QUICK TRIVIA TEST

At what age did Neymar make his professional debut?

At 17 years of age.

How many goals has he scored for Brazil?

79.

How many goals did Neymar score in his first season with Santos?

14.

What celebration gesture does he use as a tribute to his friends?

He makes a "neener neener" face.

What other sport is Neymar passionate about?

Basketball.

FIVE LIFE LESSONS

1. Perseverance is key.

No matter how great your talent, there is no guarantee that you'll achieve your goal. In Neymar's case, literally, that applied to literally scoring a goal!

However, even a miss is an opportunity to learn and improve. It takes perseverance to be the best, no matter how good your natural talent is.

2. Injury makes you stronger.

Neymar has had his fair share of injuries over the years. The 2018 foot fracture knocked him out for three months. A metatarsal injury in 2019 knocked him out for several more months. That's just two of the many injuries he has suffered.

Yet, after each injury, he came back to the beautiful game of soccer stronger, performing better than ever before. No player is happy about an injury, but the right mindset can help you come back stronger.

3. Actions have a bigger impact than you might realize.

In modern society, it's easy to post a video and have it seen by thousands of people across the globe. Neymar's influence is significantly larger, but the same basic rule applies.

How you conduct yourself has an effect on how others conduct themselves. That applies to everything you do!

4. Anything is possible!

Neymar had immense talent as a soccer player since he was young. That made it almost inevitable that he would become a professional soccer player.

However, he couldn't have known, or perhaps even dreamed, that he would get roles in movies such as "xXx: Return of Xander Cage" and "Money Heist."

Give it your all and anything is possible.

5. You can't get it right every time!

Neymar has scored some of the best goals ever seen in soccer. But, he's also missed some very easy shots—and he doesn't score every time.

That's okay. No one can be perfect all the time. It's important to fail and learn lessons from your failure. It will make it easier to succeed next time.

JUDE BELLINGHAM
YOU DON'T NEED TO LOVE
SOCCER IMMEDIATELY!

Jude Victor William Bellingham started life in Stourbridge, England. He was born in 2003, into a soccer-focused family. His father was a police officer who was well-known for scoring goals in non-league local soccer.

This meant Jude was inevitably exposed to soccer from a young age. But that doesn't mean he had an instant love for the game!

His first coach met Bellingham when the boy was four years old. He remembers putting a soccer in front of the child and finding that he had no real interest in kicking it.

His father insisted Bellingham continue to train, and the coach could see glimpses of talent. But it took several months before Bellingham developed an interest in—and eventually a love for—the game.

From there, he never looked back.

After several years at Stourbridge, Bellingham was invited to play for Birmingham City in their under-8 team. By the time he was 14, he was playing on the under-18 team, and a year later he joined the under-23 team.

When he was just 16 years and 38 days old, he officially joined the Birmingham City first team. Bellingham took the record for the youngest first-team player at Birmingham City.

Proving that one talented youngster isn't enough by themselves, his first game with Birmingham City ended in a 3-0 defeat. Despite the loss, his skills were noticed. In fact, the local Birmingham Mail called Bellingham the man of the match.

Just 19 days later, Bellingham played in his first League game, which was another defeat. But his second League appearance thrust him further into the limelight. He sat on the bench for the first hour, but after playing for 27 minutes, he noticed that the opposing keeper was under pressure and had made a mistake. Bellingham reacted instantly, diving for the ball by the goal line. He slid into it, pushing it across the line. It was the only goal in the game.

The 2019/2020 season was the only one Bellingham played for Birmingham City. By the end of the season, the new star had scored four goals and played in 44 matches. That stat may not sound impressive, but he also assisted in many of the other goals scored.

Bellingham was seen by the team and managers as an integral and essential part of the squad. He was credited as one of the main reasons Birmingham City avoided relegation that year.

It wasn't just the club that noticed his skills. Other soccer clubs in the UK and from across Europe were interested in his talents. After some negotiations, Bellingham secured a record-breaking £25 million transfer to Borussia Dortmund. It was the most expensive transfer for a 17-year-old in history.

Bellingham could have been overawed by his new club and the high-profile surroundings. Instead, he focused on the game. He started in the first match of the 2020-2021 season, and just 30 minutes in he scored his first goal.

By the end of the season, he had played in 46 games and scored four goals. His teammates voted him Newcomer of the Year.

Of course, Bellingham was still incredibly young, and competing with some of the best players in the world. It was natural that he would defer to his teammates and assist in goal-scoring. But his second season saw him score six goals, and his third season with Dortmund saw him shift up another gear, scoring an impressive 14 goals.

That was a mark of his ever-improving skills and confidence in his own abilities—something that he continues to work on. For example, he's now playing for Real Madrid. In his first 10 games for the team in the 2023-2024 season, Bellingham scored 10 goals and assisted with another three. That perfectly displays the way his game has improved and is likely to continue to do. After all, he's not even in his prime yet!

That being said, his skills are beginning to cause an issue on the field. The fans have started to notice, and this could cause real problems for Bellingham and his current team, Real Madrid. The team is relying on Bellingham to get the ball, find the space, and drive it toward or even into the goal. But when he doesn't get it right—which happens to the best of players from time to time—Real Madrid has no one else stepping up.

Bellingham was also selected as part of the England squad playing in the 2022 World Cup qualifiers. This was an impressive achievement for someone who was just 19 years old. More importantly, that decision may have saved England from being knocked out early!

Not many 19-year-olds can say they've saved England!

However, it wasn't a straightforward selection process. Thanks to the global pandemic and strict quarantine rules, Bellingham nearly wasn't released by Dortmund. Thankfully for England, a way was found to make it work.

In the game against Senegal, Bellingham really showed his skill and class. What should have been a straightforward win for the England team started out as a struggle. England wasn't playing badly, they just didn't seem coordinated or motivated. They'd only managed to score a single goal, but then Bellingham transformed the game.

It was a simple pick-up, just 40 yards from the England goal. Time seemed to pause as Bellingham looked skyward, calculating the play. He then took off with the ball, aiming for open ground. He effortlessly drifted around opponent after opponent before sending the ball perfectly to Phil Foden. A moment later, Foden passed to Harry Kane, who, perfectly positioned, drove the ball into the net. Bellingham was alongside, just in case he was needed.

It wasn't just that goal that revitalized England and led them to a 3-0 finish—it also showed how perfectly the three England midfielders worked together.

Bellingham is still learning and improving, which means there are plenty of reasons for England fans to be excited about the upcoming World Cups and other international competitions.

FUN FACTS ABOUT JUDE BELLINGHAM

- Bellingham celebrates goals by stretching out his arms with his chest out and head high.
- Bellingham was Birmingham City's youngest-ever first-team player.
- Despite playing with Birmingham City professionally for just one season, they retired his number 22 shirt when he left.
- At 18, Bellingham was already worth £67.5 million.
- His idol and inspiration is Steven Gerrard.

QUICK TRIVIA TEST

What is Bellingham's full name?

Jude Victor William Bellingham

At what age did he join the Birmingham City first team?

16 years old!

Who is Bellingham's idol?

Steven Gerrard

What position does he play?

Midfielder

Which year did Bellingham join Dortmund?

2020

FIVE LIFE LESSONS

1. Try anything.

Jude Bellingham is a gifted soccer player and a natural talent. However, when he was first introduced to soccer, he wasn't that interested. He tried it anyway, and eventually, his passion for the sport grew. Now he loves playing, proving that it's worth it to try anything. You never know where it might lead.

2. Age isn't important.

Jude Bellingham proved that this is true. At just 19, he was selected to play for England.

He's not the youngest player to receive this honor, but it still shows that age doesn't matter. You're never too old or young to try.

3. Remember that you're a role model.

It's easy to see celebrities as role models because millions of people see what they do and imitate them. That's certainly true of Bellingham. His fans are known for copying his haircut and even the vibrant colors he dyes it.

As a role model, he needs to be aware of how his actions will be viewed and affect others.

You don't need to be rich and famous to influence other people. Remember that the next time you are considering doing something foolish or dangerous. You never know who is watching and imitating you.

4. You don't have to be an extrovert.

Jude Bellingham has a huge amount of energy. That's true today, and it was true he was young. His teachers, friends, and family can all confirm this.

But you may be surprised to learn that he's not exceptionally outgoing. Bellingham is known to be reserved, proving that you can still make your dreams come true, regardless of your personality.

5. Be a team player.

There are soccer greats who could take a ball and run it down the entire field to score, but most great players realize that working as a team is better. That's what Bellingham has shown himself capable of doing on multiple occasions.

Remember, it's much easier to find success as part of a team.

KAKA
PLAYING AFTER A SPINAL INJURY

Although he may be known as Ricardo Kaka, the full name of one of South America's greatest soccer success stories is Ricardo Izecson dos Santos Leite. He was born in Brazil in April of 1982.

Both of his parents worked, allowing him to receive a good education and develop his love for and skill in soccer.

Even when he was young, Kaka was known for being surprisingly level-headed. As a result, his school allowed him to play soccer— and when they saw his natural talent, they got him a spot in the local club known as Alphaville.

Thanks to his dedication and natural skill, Kaka's club made it to the finals of a local competition. That led to him receiving a place in the youth academy at San Paulo FC, which was located in the town he lived in with his parents. He was just eight at the time.

Seven years later, after years of impressive dribbling, passing, and ball control, San Paulo FC offered to sign him properly. He was just 15 when he made his first appearance for the team.

Despite his young age and playing with people who were older and more experienced, he didn't really struggle. In fact, this challenge inspired Kaka to shine. It helped him improve as a team member, and eventually, his skills attracted attention from other clubs.

He appeared 27 times in his first season, scoring 12 goals. In his second season, he scored 10 goals in just 20 appearances. An array of European clubs were suddenly interested in signing him.

Interestingly, he nearly didn't make his first season. In 2000, when his talents were already more than obvious, Kaka had an accident in his swimming pool. He came down a water slide, but the water wasn't deep enough. He hit the bottom of the pool. The result was a fractured vertebra in his spine. In the hospital, it wasn't initially clear whether he would end up paralyzed or with a career-ending injury.

Fortunately, his young body dealt with the injury and healed completely. Of course, the accident stopped him from playing for several months, but his dedication to fitness and training meant he was still ready to play with the first team by January 2001.

He scored in his first game for the San Paulo senior and later led the team in taking the Torneio Rio-Sao Paulo Championships. It was the first time the team had ever won it!

It was obvious that Kaka had a bright and promising future, and several European clubs saw the potential in him. AC Milan made the first move. Realizing that this was a great opportunity to improve his skills, Kaka immediately signed with Milan.

Unlike so many before him, Kaka didn't struggle after moving to a big European club. Instead, he jumped at the challenge. In his first season with AC Milan, he scored 10 goals and demonstrated his impressive skills over and over again. His contribution helped Milan win the Serie A in his first season, a result that was directly attributed to Kaka, as he delivered the essential cross to Shevchenko, which gave them the winning goal.

His performance earned him the Serie A Player of the Year award. He was also nominated for the Ballon d'Or and FIFA World Player of the Year. Later in his career, Kaka actually won the Ballon d'Or in 2007, becoming recognized as the greatest player in the world for that year.

Although 2007 was particularly special for Kaka, 2006 was perhaps the lowest point in his career. The 2006 World Cup was an exciting prospect for Brazil, as they were seen as favorites to win. After all, they had four fantastic attackers: Ronaldinho, Ronaldo, Adriano, and Kaka.

At that time, Brazil was one of the favorites to win the tournament. Unfortunately, the team didn't give it their all. Some were more interested in sampling the nightlife in the host country Germany. Others simply underperformed.

As a result, the team lost to France in the quarterfinals and were sent home. It was a stark contrast to Brazil's experience winning the World Cup in 2002, with a little help from Kaka. He debuted for the Brazilian national team in 2002 and played for 25 minutes in the first round. Brazil won 5-2 against Costa Rica giving Kaka a taste of success. It allowed him to say he was a small part of the Brazil World Cup success.

After bouncing back from that disappointment, Kaka enjoyed his golden years from 2007–2010. He would probably say that 2009 was his favorite season, as Brazil won the Confederations Cup that year. Brazil had already won the cup in 2005, and, thanks to Kaka, they held onto it again in 2009.

Kaka performed magnificently in the tournament. He scored two goals and two assists, and his ball-handling skills were unmatched. At the end of the tournament, he was awarded the Golden Ball, signifying he was the best player on the field.

He played for Brazil again in 2010 as they tried to win the World Cup. Unfortunately, although the team played much better than in 2006, they lost to the Netherlands in the quarterfinals.

Sadly, this was the last time Kaka played for the Brazilian squad. Due to a series of injuries and coaching changes, he was never able to play, despite being frequently selected.

Because of the injuries he sustained while playing for Real Madrid, it became impossible for him to burst forward explosively with the ball, which made it significantly harder for Kaka to punch through the midfield and create goal-scoring opportunities.

Kaka's career at Real Madrid started well, and his first season was impressive. However, in August 2010, he had surgery for a knee problem and ended up on the bench for eight months.

He returned with confidence and quickly made his mark again, but in March of 2011, he had another knee injury, causing him to be sidelined for roughly a month.

Again, he returned triumphantly, helping Real Madrid to another win. In fact, that year he was named the best player of the Champions League Matchday. But he wasn't happy at Madrid, and after four years he returned to AC Milan.

Further injuries limited his ability to shine at Milan. He went on to play for several other teams until 2017 when he officially retired from the game.

Kaka was undoubtedly one of the most talented, down-to-earth players to ever grace the field, and proof that hard work pays off. As he said, "I'm not the most talented, but I am the most professional."

FUN FACTS ABOUT RICARDO KAKA

- He received the nickname Kaka because his younger brother couldn't pronounce his name properly.
- In February of 2007, he became an Italian citizen.
- Kaka married his childhood sweetheart in 2005, and they stayed married for 10 years.
- He was the first sportsperson to have 10 million Twitter followers.
- Kaka played 654 and scored 208 goals at club level.

QUICK TRIVIA TEST

What is Ricardo Kaka's real name?

Ricardo Izecson dos Santos Leite.

When was Ricardo Kaka born?

April 1982.

Which year did Kaka and the Brazil squad win the World Cup?

2002.

How much did AC Milan pay for Kaka in 2003?

€8.8 million.

Which year did he win the Ballon d'Or?

2007.

FIVE LIFE LESSONS

1. Accidents happen.

Kaka slid down a waterslide and hit his head on the bottom of a swimming pool. It was an injury that could have paralyzed him, yet he made a full recovery.

Accidents happen, but that shouldn't make you afraid to do something, just take the appropriate safety measures first.

2. Courage is essential in life

Courage is the act of doing something even if you're afraid, it's not the absence of fear. Kaka believed that courage was an essential part of his journey to success.

As he said, "You need this courage or you will never create something different from the others."

3. Give it your all every time.

Kaka was part of a group of attackers that everyone feared, and they were the reason that Brazil was a favorite to win the 2006 World Cup.

He acknowledges that he wasn't the most talented of the four, but he was the most professional. His discipline and willingness to give it all, every time, allowed him to stand tall amongst the most talented players in the world.

4. Stay true to yourself.

Kaka is a devout Christian. He was known for praying before games and thanking God for goals, amongst other things. He never shied away from telling others about his beliefs, but did so without pressuring them to believe the same as him.

That's a good attitude for anyone to have.

5. Life is full of ups and downs.

In December 2012, Kaka scored a goal in the 49th minute against Ajax. This gave him 28 goals and made him the top goal-scorer in the Champions League. But less than 40 days later, he was sent off while playing against C.A. Osasuna as a result of him being booked twice in just 18 minutes.

The fall from such a high to a disappointing low reminded him that everything has its ups and downs. Make the most of the highs, and they'll carry you through the lows.

CHRISTIANO RONALDO POVERTY AND HEART DISEASE

Christiano Ronaldo dos Santos Aveiro was born in February 1985. He grew up in poverty. His father was working two jobs and barely making ends meet. Portugal had just lost a war against Angola, and the country was in a financial crisis.

In fact, when his mom got pregnant, his parents actually decided to abort the baby, but the doctor denied them that opportunity. Instead, one of the greatest soccer players the world has ever seen was born.

Of course, everyone in the country was in a similar situation at the time, so children played soccer in the streets because it was free. Most were good players, but, even from a young age, Ronaldo stood out. He could outplay children several years older than him.

His first break came at age 12. His talent had been noticed, and Sporting CP wanted him. But, if he wanted to play, he would have to move to Lisbon. That's a tough challenge for a 12-year-old kid.

At 14, he decided to drop out of school and commit himself to chasing a career in professional soccer.

A year later, he was diagnosed with racing heart syndrome. His options were surgery or to stop playing soccer. As far as Ronaldo was concerned, there was no choice.

His dedication saw him practicing after training was finished for the day and even practicing in the forest, simply because it was more challenging.

The hard work (and natural skill) paid off. When he turned 16, he could play professionally, so he played for Sporting CP. He played in the under-16, under-17, under-18, B team, and first team—all in the same season!

When he was 18 years old, Sporting played Manchester United in a friendly. The Man United players were so impressed with Ronaldo that they demanded their boss, Sir Alex Ferguson, sign him.

A few days later, Ronaldo became the first Portuguese player to play for Manchester United. Although Ronaldo requested the number 28 jersey, his potential was so obvious that he was given the number 7—the same jersey legends like David Beckham, George Best, and Eric Cantona wore.

Ronaldo's debut game was like a dream. He performed brilliantly, using his full bag of tricks, flicks, and stepovers, all with typical Ronaldo flair. The fans instantly fell in love with him.

However, despite his obvious skill, Ronaldo was still a little rough around the edges. In the first three seasons at Manchester United, he scored just 19 goals. To put that in context, he has scored more than that per season for at least 13 seasons in his career.

The lack of finish and the fact that Manchester United didn't win any League titles for the first three years of his time with them led people to think he was a "one-trick pony," and that he couldn't handle the pressure of the Premier League.

Of course, we now know how wrong these people were!

The 2006 World Cup transformed Ronaldo. Before the World Cup, most people saw him as a lightweight winger. More importantly, he was an entertainer on the field.

It was this that led to him getting Rooney sent off and winking to the crowd. It made him unpopular with the fans. The good news was that this made him think long and hard about his game and what he wanted to achieve.

Alongside bulking up, he dropped the entertainer persona and started focusing on winning. His skills developed as he used directness and sought to be efficient. The result was a player who became known as one of the deadliest attackers in the world.

The result was 64 goals in 101 Premier League games. Ronaldo had found himself, and Manchester United reaped the benefits. This included winning the Champions League by beating Chelsea.

In 2008, in recognition of his superb skill, Ronaldo was given the Ballon d'Or, the FIFA World Player of the Year, and the European Golden Shoe.

This was the same year that Ronaldo was pushing for a transfer to Real Madrid, the club he had always wanted to play for. However, Manchester United retained Ronaldo for one more season.

It's interesting to note that the 2009 Champions League final was Manchester United against Barcelona, a Spanish team. Manchester United lost, marking the only time Ronaldo had lost a Champions League final—and at the same time, he wanted to transfer to Spain.

This certainly raised eyebrows. A short time later, Real Madrid paid an impressive £80 million for Ronaldo.

It was a good investment for Real Madrid. During his nine seasons with the team, Ronaldo played an impressive 438 games. More impressively, he scored 450 goals. That's more than one goal a game, making Ronaldo Real Madrid's top goal scorer of all time.

Real Madrid won 16 trophies while Ronaldo played for them, more than any other decade in history. Ronaldo also picked up four Ballon d'Or's and three European Golden Shoes during this time.

Ronaldo barely put a foot wrong during this period. It's not surprising that Real Madrid got £100 million when they transferred him to Juventus.

Juventus was prepared to pay so much because Ronaldo's reputation as a deadly center-forward was enough to strike fear into the hearts of anyone.

His performance at Juventus was similar to his early years at Real Madrid. He dominated the left wing and continued to build his reputation as a prolific goal scorer.

In time, Juventus began to struggle, and Ronaldo couldn't carry an entire team by himself. This prompted a move back to Manchester United in 2021, and the start of a low point in his career.

Despite being one of the best players in the world, Ronaldo wasn't allowed to start every game. He almost single-handedly got Manchester United to the knockout stages of the 2021-2022 Champions League, but a struggling team and a less-than-supportive coach meant Ronaldo quickly grew unhappy.

Fortunately, Ronaldo has found one more place to shine. Early in 2023, he signed a contract to play in the Saudi Pro League. Ronaldo feels he has done everything he can in Europe, and this offers him a new challenge.

In addition, it will do wonders for the Saudi Pro League, attracting a lot of positive attention and proving that one man can make a difference.

FUN FACTS ABOUT CHRISTIANO RONALDO

- His father named him Ronaldo after American president Ronald Reagan.
- He has six children!
- Ronaldo's friend, Albert Fantrau, sacrificed his soccer dream to give Ronaldo his chance at the soccer academy.
- He can jump higher than the average NBA player!
- There's a museum in Maderia dedicated to his trophies.

QUICK TRIVIA TEST

What is Ronaldo's full name?

Christiano Ronaldo dos Santos Aveiro

How many Ballon d'Or's has he won?

Five

How many seasons did Ronaldo play with Real Madrid?

Nine

Why did Manchester United decide to buy him?

Sir Alex Ferguson was impressed watching him play in a friendly against Manchester United.

Where did he go after playing for Juventus?

Back to Manchester United

FIVE LIFE LESSONS

1. Live your dream.

Ever since he was young, Ronaldo wanted to be a professional soccer player. His natural skill and dedication made this possible, even after discovering he had a heart problem.

As he says, "I'm living a dream I never want to wake up from."

Choose your dream and go for it. Anything is possible.

2. Always maintain a strong work ethic.

There is no doubt that Ronaldo has natural talent. However, that's not enough by itself. He was good in his first three seasons at Manchester United, but not world-beating. It was only after the 2006 World Cup, when he found himself and the right work ethic, that he became the legend he now is.

He's proof that if you work hard and maintain your work ethic, anything is possible.

3. Give it your all.

If you want to get to the top, you need to give it your all. Focus on your goal, train for it, and seize any opportunity you can.

If you give it your all, anything is possible.

4. Staying at the top is much harder than getting there.

It almost seems like Ronaldo was destined to be the best soccer player in the world, so it's not surprising that he won so many Ballon d'Or's and other awards.

However, as he'll tell you, staying at the top is much harder than getting there.

Once you're at the top, you're constantly under pressure. People know what you can deliver, and expect it every time. Remember that as you climb to the top.

5. Focus on fitness.

By most definitions, Ronaldo is past his prime. His game should be in decline, as he is now on the wrong side of 30.

However, because he has remained focused on his fitness, he is still capable of beating players 10 years younger than him.

I have included these free downloadable gifts to help light up your inner inspiration & reach your potential.

While you are reading through the stories, lessons and trivia, we recommend that you make use of all the bonuses we've attached here!

All our bonuses have been made specifically to help young athletes feel fired up, get inspired from the best to ever do it, and most importantly fall more in love with this incredible game!

Here's a list of what you're getting:

1) 250 Fun Facts From The World Of Sports
2) Sports Practice and Game Calendar
3) 5 Fun Exercise Drills for Kids
4) The BEST Advice From The Greatest Athletes Of All Time
5) The Mental Mindset Guided Meditation & Affirmation Collection
6) The Most Famous Events In Sports History And What They Can Teach Us

Now, it's over to you to scan the QR code, follow the instructions & get started!

MOHAMED SALAH
VILLAGE KID TURNED GLOBAL SUPERSTAR

Mohamed Salah was born in Egypt in June of 1992. At the time of his birth, no one knew that he would go on to become a legend. Today, he's generally considered one of the best players currently active and one of the greatest African soccer players of all time. However, his beginnings were very humble.

He was born and grew up in a small Egyptian village called Nagrig with his siblings. He spent much of his time with his brother Nasr. They both had a love of soccer from a young age. In fact, this love ran in the family. Two of his uncles and his father had all played in the local youth club.

Salah's talent was quickly spotted, allowing him to join the El Mokawloon youth team and further his training and experience. He was just 14 at the time, but as soon as he reached 18, he was signed by the senior team. His play at the local level quickly brought more attention, and the Swiss club FC Basel signed him in 2012 when he was just 20.

In his first season with the club, he helped them to win the Swiss Super League. He also received the Swiss Golden Player Award.

His two-year stint at FC Basel also included several European Soccer Association games, which was great for his exposure.

Thanks to Salah's consistent, high-quality play, Chelsea FC became interested in the rising star. He eventually transferred to one of the best Premier League teams in the world. It was a transfer that nearly didn't happen as Salah could have been forced to return to Egypt for military service at any time. That would have meant a big risk for Chelsea, paying a large transfer fee and then losing their player for two years. Fortunately, the Egyptian government gave him a pass.

Unfortunately, this is where things got difficult for Salah. The English culture and expectations were significantly different to his Egyptian origins, and even to his time at FC Basel.

His play suffered, as did his confidence. The club had high expectations, but Salah struggled to meet them.

As a result, he played in just six matches with Chelsea before they loaned him to Fiorentina, a team in Italy's top soccer league.

It was this move that helped Salah find his own path. The move reduced the pressure on him, and the team environment was more understanding, reassuring, and helpful.

Florentina allowed him to play his own way, and that built his confidence.

Unfortunately, Chelsea still wasn't convinced of his skills. After his stint at Florentina, Chelsea loaned Salah to AS Roma, another Italian team in their top league.

AC Roma was impressed with Salah, and they made a bid for him. Salah's transfer was confirmed before the 2016-2017 season officially started. During that season, Salah scored 19 goals and assisted with another 13. The team named him Player of the Year. His perseverance to find the right team had finally paid off.

Salah played just one season for Roma, but it was enough to transform his potential into reality.

In July 2017, he played his first Premier League game for Liverpool, and the difference from his Chelsea debut was obvious. Salah could dribble a ball at speed across almost the entire field, and still find an opening to get the ball into the back of the net.

His 2017-2018 season was awesome. Salah scored 32 goals in 38 games. In the process, he took the Premier League record for most goals in one season.

Salah was also instrumental in getting Liverpool to the UEFA Champions League final. They lost it to Real Madrid, but Salah won the European Golden Boot.

That wasn't the only time he won the Golden Boot. He took it again in the 2018-2019 season, and then again in the 2021-2022 season.

In May of 2018, he also won the Premier League's Player of the Season. No Egyptian had ever won this award before, and only two Liverpool players have had the honor!

Naturally, Salah also played for his national team. His first appearance with the squad was in 2011 when he was just 19. While his contributions in the first few years were valuable, he was still finding himself.

As he came to be the highly skilled and experienced player we know today, his influence had a profound effect on the team. Salah led Egypt to the finals of the 2017 Africa Cup of Nations (although they lost 2-1 to Cameroon).

He did the same in 2021, bringing Egypt to the final again, Where they were beaten by Senegal.

That same year, he was instrumental in Egypt qualifying for the World Cup. It's worth noting that this was the first time Egypt had ever made it to a World Cup.

Like any player, Salah has known defeat on the field. But, he is also responsible for some of the most impressive soccer moments in the last 10 years.

One great example of how Salah has come together as a person and a player was his impossible goal against Palermo in 2016. At the time, he was playing for Roma.

Salah was positioned in the box, ready to receive. Unfortunately, the ball came in hard, forcing his first touch to be heavy. The ball bounced around the advancing keeper and toward the goal line. With lightning speed, Salah got around the ball and, instead of passing it back, curled a shot toward the goal.

The ball bounced just off the goal line and spun straight into the back of the net.

Salah has not yet reached his prime, but there is little doubt he has transformed from an inexperienced and uncertain forward to arguably one of the best in the world. And he still has time to develop and improve.

He also has time to take Egypt further in the World Cup, and win the Africa Cup of Nations.

This is a man who has come a long way, but his journey isn't over yet.

FUN FACTS ABOUT MOHAMED SALAH

- Salah scored 5 goals for Egypt in the 2018 World Cup.
- He was discovered at 14 by a scout, although the scout was supposed to be watching someone else.
- He became part of a senior club at just 15, and needed a special diet and training program.
- Salah married his high school girlfriend in 2013.
- He was the first player to score 100 goals for Liverpool since Steven Gerrard.

QUICK TRIVIA TEST

Where was Salah born?

Egypt.

How many brothers and sisters does he have?

Two.

Why was he loaned to Fiorentina?

Salah was struggling at Chelsea.

What event almost caused the cancellation of his transfer to Chelsea?

It was suggested he could be forced to return to Egypt for military service

How many seasons did Salah play for Roma?

Just one

FIVE LIFE LESSONS

1. Find what works for you.

Salah was an excellent player at Sporting, but he struggled at Chelsea. The difference in culture hit him hard.

However, he persevered and worked out how to handle the issues, allowing him to reach his full potential.

2. Commit to being the best version of you.

His managers have said that Salah always gives his all. If he's asked to be at training at a certain time, he'll always be there an hour before to practice and make the most of the opportunity.

He has worked hard to reach the top, and continues to do so. This is because he's committed to being the best version of himself possible.

3. Be Prepared

Salah is quoted as saying "I keep my focus on the team and concentrate on the best possible match preparations."

Despite his skill, Salah believes that you need to work hard, stay focused, and be prepared to succeed. It works for him!

4. Visualize success.

When Salah was struggling at Chelsea, he still knew he wanted to be one of the top soccer players in the world.

One trick he used to help him get there was to visualize himself succeeding. It worked for him, just as it has worked for many other people. If you have a goal and visualize yourself successfully reaching it, you'll find it will help.

5. Everyone gets it wrong sometimes

Even the best players in the world can get it wrong sometimes. Playing soccer means you're part of a team. You need to play as part of a team, both on and off the field.

As Salah says "I miss many chances, but I always keep trying."

ANTOINE GRIEZMANN
OVERCOMING FAILURE

Antoine Griezmann was born on March 21, 1991, in Saône-et-Loire, France. His father's family had moved to France from Germany in the early part of the 19th century, and his mother was of Portuguese descent.

His childhood was relatively normal, although they spent most holidays in Portugal at Pacos de Ferreira, where his grandfather had played professional soccer.

Like many children, Griezmann grew up playing soccer on the streets. His talents were obvious from a young age, which led to him joining the club in his home town: UF Mâconnais.

This was where he encountered his first challenge. Griezmann was shorter and slimmer than most of his peers. While he had excellent ball skills, he tried out for several youth academies and was rejected. Each one found a bigger and stronger player more appealing.

Undeterred, Griezmann continued to train and play. He eventually got a trial spot with Montpellier, which led to his big break.

He played one of the best games of his young career during a friendly against Paris Saint-Germain youth academy. As fate would have it, several scouts were watching, including those from Real Sociedad.

The scouts were so impressed that, as soon as the match finished, they offered Griezmann a one-week trial. It didn't matter that this meant moving to San Sebastian, Spain. Griezmann seized the opportunity.

One week turned into two, and then he was offered a youth contract. His parents needed to be convinced that their 14-year-old son would be okay in Spain, but they fortunately agreed.

Griezmann is now recognized as one of the most talented players of his generation, yet his official debut for the club resulted in a 2-0 defeat. That being said, he didn't come on until the 77th minute, which means there was little he could have done to transform the game.

Losing your first official game is an excellent way to get motivated for the future. Griezmann tasted failure and knew he would have to work even harder to succeed.

Just a few days later, he made his official League debut. However, he didn't really make his mark for another three weeks, when he started a game against Huesca and scored his first goal, helping the team to a 2-0 victory!

He went on to score more goals in October and November. In one match, he was the only goal scorer. That was enough to ensure that he was selected for every match for the rest of the season.

To finish his inspirational start as a professional soccer player, he helped Real Sociedad win the League and get promoted to La Liga.

Unsurprisingly, at the end of the season, he was offered a professional contract. Although he had received several offers from French clubs, and even another Basque club, he signed with Real Sociedad for five years.

His professional League debut went well. Griezmann described it as fulfilling his childhood dream. He scored or assisted in the first eight games of the season. Griezmann then endured a nine-match run without a goal, possibly the longest stretch of his entire career.

Again, this was an excellent learning experience. During that period, Griezmann learned a lot about the tactics and strategies that lead to goals.

Griezmann was soon back to scoring, gaining notice for the way in which he could put a goal together, rather than simply drive the ball into the net.

This led to Atletico Madrid making an offer for Griezmann. After the standard negotiation and medical, Griezmann signed with Atletico on July 29, 2014.

Just two weeks later, he debuted for the club. It took another month for him to score his first goal, and the team actually lost that match to Olympiacos—but he was just getting started.

By November, Griezmann appeared to have settled into his new club. His brace in the November 1 game against Cordoba was quickly followed by a hat trick against Athletic Bilbao.

Over the next two years, Griezmann's scoring finesse improved dramatically. His skills in 2016 saw him lead Atletico through the qualifiers with two matches to spare. He nearly won the Ballon d'Or that year, coming third after Ronaldo and Messi.

By the end of the 2016-2017 season, he had scored 100 goals in La Liga, becoming only the second Frenchman to ever do this. However, he still hadn't won a trophy of his own.

Antoine Griezmann had consistently scored goals and helped his team win vital victories. However, in July 2019, Barcelona agreed to pay his $120 million buy-out clause, and two weeks later, he was playing for his new team.

Despite scoring goals at Barcelona, this was a dark period for Griezmann. The move itself caused issues, as Atletico believed the buy-out should have been $200 million. In addition, the Barcelona fans offered Griezmann a lukewarm reception. They were annoyed that he had pulled out of a transfer the previous season. In addition, some fans simply felt that Griezmann couldn't replace Neymar.

Unfortunately, they were ultimately proved right. Barcelona tried to use Griezmann in the same position and the same types of play that Neymar had loved. However, Griezmann is a second striker, and his skills weren't the same as Neymar's.

Neymar could handle a wide range of plays from wide arrays, while Griezmann offered some of the best finishes in Europe and was fantastic at using half-spaces to establish creative plays. But Barcelona's Ernesto Valverde put Griezmann on the left wing, leaving him struggling to do anything positive for the team.

Once again, Griezmann was faced with an incredibly difficult challenge. He couldn't create imaginative plays, he was frequently ignored on the wing (including his runs up field), and he would frequently have to aid with defense. That left him nowhere near the attacking position he needed to be in to make a difference.

By the end of the season, the fans were calling for Griezmann to be let go. At this stage, he was close to 30 and his career seemed to be winding down.

The following season, a coaching change didn't help Griezmann. He was switched to the other flank, but still far from his favorite and customary position. Six games into the season, he didn't have a goal to his name.

Griezmann could have given up. Instead, he voiced his concerns, telling everyone of the troubles he had faced from various coaches. Speaking up for himself and his newfound focus helped. In his first three games that January, he scored three goals—and one was potentially the best goal of the season by any player.

The transformation continued as Griezmann made the most of his position. By the end of the season, he had more goals than Cristiano Ronaldo—impressive, for a player some called the "Barcelona Flop."

Despite Griezmann's apparent return to form, he still wasn't happy at Barcelona. Griezmann had scored just 22 goals in 74 La Liga games. It was almost inevitable that he would move on.

What surprised everyone was his loan by Barcelona back to Atletico, with an obligation to buy for €40 million. That was significantly less than the €120 million Barcelona had paid for him!

The move was just what Griezmann needed. Atletico welcomed him back on their own terms, and he played like he had never left.

His wife had once said to him, "If you go to Barcelona, you will be just another player. At Atletico, you will be history." She was right. At Barcelona, Griezmann was just another player—one who didn't get the position he needed to shine. His return to Atletico instantly allowed him to succeed. It led to perhaps his most defining moment, when he scored his 173rd goal, matching Atletico's greatest player, "Big Boots" Luis Aragones, whose statue stands proudly outside the club.

FUN FACTS ABOUT ANTOINE GRIEZMANN

- He left home at 13, after accepting an offer from a Spanish club.
- As a child, he enjoyed both scoring goals and being a goalkeeper.
- Griezmann loves the NBA. His favorite player is Derrick Rose.
- Griezmann is the voice of Superman in the French version of Batman: The Lego Movie.
- He discovered he was third for the Ballon d'Or while driving.

QUICK TRIVIA TEST

Which club did Griezmann play for first?

Real Sociedad.

Why was Griezmann turned down by most soccer academies?

His small size and lightweight frame.

How old was he when he moved to Spain?

14.

Why did he struggle at Barcelona?

He was never allowed to play in his preferred position.

Whose record at Atletico did he match?

"Big Boots" Luis Aragones.

FIVE LIFE LESSONS

1. There's no place like home, so appreciate what you have.

Antoine Griezmann excelled at Atletico, but he struggled at Barcelona, despite being one of the best players in the world.

The truth is, the grass isn't always greener elsewhere. Sometimes it's best to appreciate what you have.

2. Keep trying.

Griezmann's stint at Barcelona was difficult. However, while he struggled in the wrong position, he still kept trying.

Ultimately, he scored more goals than anyone else, proving that trying makes anything possible.

3. Avoid assumptions.

It would seem fair to assume that Griezmann, one of the best players in the world, would excel at Barcelona. However, this assumption proves you shouldn't assume anything.

He's a versatile and naturally gifted player, but Barcelona was already struggling, and Griezmann didn't get the support he needed to excel. His period at Barcelona nearly cost him his reputation.

4. Follow your dreams.

As a child, Griezmann was smaller and slimmer than everyone else. That meant that many soccer academies passed over him.

He persevered and stuck to his dreams, even when it meant moving to a different country by himself. Following that dream paid off.

5. Support those you love.

A lot has been said about Griezmann and the way he rose above challenges to become one of the best players in the world.

However, little is said about the level of support he received from every member of his family. Without them, he would never have made it to the top.

If you make it big in any field, remember those that helped you get there.

LUKA MODRIC
LIVING AS A REFUGEE

Luka Modric was born in Croatia in September 1985. As a child, he lived in a small village on the mountain slopes. His parents worked in a knitwear factory, which meant that the young boy spent most of his time with his grandfather.

By the time he was five years old, he was accomplished at shepherding goats. Unfortunately, the Croatian War of Independence started, his grandfather was murdered, their house was burned to the ground, and they had to flee, becoming refugees.

Despite the fact that bombs were falling daily, Modric's parents tried to give him a normal upbringing. He made friends and played soccer on the war-torn streets.

When he was seven, he started primary school and attended a sporting academy. It was instantly obvious that the young Modric had talent. This earned him a place in various training camps.

However, despite his potential, Modric was very light. This was enough to put off the biggest clubs in the region, especially Hajduk Split.

Modric continued to dedicate his time to the sport and was eventually accepted by Dinamo Zagreb when he was 16 years old. He played well for them for a season, which earned him a loan to Zrinjski Mostar, a team in the Bosnian Premier League.

It was here that Modric really started to shine, earning the Bosnian League Player of the Year award.

Modric's tough childhood helped him stay grounded after signing his first long-term contract in 2005. He signed with Dinamo Zagreb for 10 years and bought a flat for his family.

During his first season, he played regularly for the first team and helped them win the League. Modric scored 7 goals in 31 matches.

His second season at Dinamo Zagreb produced similar results. The team again won the League, and Modric's contribution was invaluable, as he was the player who would feed their striker, Eduardo, the ball.

In his third season, the team tried to qualify for the UEFA Cup. They enjoyed several successes on the field, but ultimately failed to move beyond the group stage.

After four seasons with Dinamo Zagreb, Modric had 31 goals and 29 assists. He started to get attention from other clubs, including Barcelona, Chelsea, and Arsenal.

In 2008, Modric accepted an offer from Tottenham Hotspur. It was a record transfer fee for the club of £16.5 million.

Modric went from being the big fish in a little pond to just another fish in a much larger pond. His first game at Tottenham was a 2-1 defeat to Middlesbrough.

In addition to having to settle into a much bigger scene and adjusting to England's cultural differences, Modric suffered a knee injury, hampering his ability to play. Plus, many in the League described him as a lightweight—something that Modric denied. He may have been small, but he was mentally and physically tough.

Despite that fact, his woes on the field continued as he was moved through several different positions. His teammates acknowledged that Modric's versatility was both a blessing and a curse. Playing different positions probably helped his overall game, but he never had time to thrive in one position.

After a poor season, and with Tottenham questioning the value of the transfer, a new manager was appointed to the team. Harry Redknapp took over and moved Modric into central midfielder, sometimes left midfielder. This was the role Modric was born for, and the improvement in his play was instantaneous.

He immediately seemed to be more in control of the ball and the team, directing play and securing a 4-4 draw with Tottenham's arch-rival, Arsenal. Redknapp could see Modric's skills and built his new team around him.

That's when things turned around for Modric. He started scoring goals, and Tottenham started moving up the League standings.

In 2010, Tottenham finished fourth in the League, and there were signs of more to come. Modric signed a six-year contract with the team, stating that, despite offers from other Premier League teams, Tottenham was where he wanted to be.

To prove the point, he helped the team get into the UEFA Champions League for the first time ever. They made it as far as the quarterfinals, and Modric was voted Tottenham Hotspur's player of the year, something that several other top clubs said they agreed with.

At this stage, Modric was interested in playing with another London club. Several offers were made, but they were all turned down by Tottenham. Frustrated, Modric refused to play the first game of the season, leading to Redknapp to have a stern word with him, telling him to "get his head in the game."

The 2011-2012 season saw him score several goals and assists, but there were those who questioned whether the magic had gone. Then, in 2012, he transferred to Real Madrid, where he sat on the bench. Real Madrid already had established midfielders, and he was brought on as a substitute. With limited opportunity to shine, Modric was voted worst signing of the year by the Spanish newspaper Marca.

Once again, Modric found himself adjusting to a new culture, trying to find the right spot on a team, and having to prove that he was worth the investment.

Modric turned it all around in March of 2013. Real Madrid was playing Manchester United in the Champions League and was behind by a goal. Modric seized the opportunity late in the first half. He created space and shot the ball into the back of the net from 25 yards out.

His play became transformative for the rest of the game, carrying Madrid to a 2-1 victory. More importantly, it transformed the way he played for Real Madrid.

From that moment on, he became instrumental to Madrid's success, creating opportunities, feeding strikers, scoring occasionally, and becoming the most accurate passer on the field.

Between 2013 and 2015, Modric had 90% accuracy in passing. He was also heavily involved in beating Barcelona 2-1 to take the 2013-2014 Copa del Rey.

During this period, he received the LFP award for best midfielder and was included in the UEFA Champions Team.

Modric's game had improved since, and it was only getting better. The team and the manager relied on him to put the ball in the right place, and the fans now adored him.

After 2015, Modric continued to win an array of awards, both individually and for his team. Of particular merit was the Ballon d'Or in December of 2018. This was also the year that Modric led Croatia to the World Cup final. The team played against France and lost 4-2, but they fought like lions and Modric's performance earned him the Golden Ball as player of the tournament.

Today, Modric is regarded as one of the greatest players ever to grace the field. Not bad for a child who was herding goats at just five years old. The fact that Real Madrid signed a new contract with him when he was 38 years old, shows that this amazing story isn't over yet.

FUN FACTS ABOUT LUKA MODRIC

- Modric states that Carlo Ancelotti was the best manager he played under.
- Vedran Corluka was the best man at Modric's wedding.
- He was named Euro 2016 Refugee XI by FARE.
- His idol is Ronaldo.
- Barcelona passed on signing Modric—a fact that they later regretted.

QUICK TRIVIA TEST

Why was Modric a refugee?

The Croatian War of Independence made him and his family homeless.

When did he sign with Tottenham Hotspur?

2008.

Which year did he win the Ballon d'Or?

2018.

How many goals and assists did he get in four seasons with Dinamo Zagreb?

31 goals and 29 assists.

What did the local Spanish newspaper say about him after his first season at Real Madrid?

The worst signing of the year.

FIVE LIFE LESSONS

1. Anything is possible.

Modric was smaller than most children and overlooked by local teams. he could have given up. Instead, he kept doing what he loved, waited for his opportunity, and proved that anything is possible.

He started as a refugee with nothing, and has since taken Croatia to the final of the World Cup!

2. Push your boundaries.

It would have been easy for Modric to stay at the club level in Bosnia. However, he pushed to get into the Premier League. In the process, he pushed his boundaries.

Twice in his career, he has needed to make huge cultural shifts, requiring him to embrace new teams and local traditions.

His approach has worked, proving that it's good to push your boundaries.

3. Hard work pays off.

Modric has endured hard times. His start at Tottenham and even his start at Real Madrid were both shaky. But both of his coaches noted that he was prepared to work hard and that he was dedicated to the success of the team. His hard work paid off, and today he is considered one of the best soccer players in the world.

4. Take care of your family.

When Modric got his first long-term contract, he immediately purchased a flat for his family to live in. This was a reminder to them that their sacrifices were part of his success.

5. Practice makes perfect.

Modric is a talented player. However, much of his skill comes from practice and experience. He can visualize plays, knows where to put the ball, and ensures his teammates are in the right position to finish.

It takes skill and practice to get this right nearly every time.

KARIM BENZEMA
LEAVING GANGLIFE BEHIND

Karim Benzema is best known as a striker for the French international soccer team. He's also the captain of Al-Ittihad, a club in the Saudi Pro League.

To many, he is one of the best strikers of all time. He has real vision on the field, finding creative plays and creating goal opportunities. He's also incredibly versatile.

To illustrate how good he is, Benzema is the second-highest goal scorer of all time for Real Madrid!

He's won a staggering 25 trophies while playing with Real Madrid. That includes four for winning the La Liga, five for winning the UEFA Champions League, and three Copa del Reya titles.

This all sounds amazing, like the sort of player anyone would want to be. But it hasn't all been easy for the soccer star!

Benzema was born in 1987 in Lyon, France. His upbringing was pretty standard, similar to many other children in the city. He played soccer where he could, and seemed to have a natural talent. His two younger brothers also displayed talent.

Unfortunately, the area he lived in was full of gangs. It was only his father's strict discipline that prevented the young boy from joining one and taking a very different path in life.

Benzema's local club, AS Bron Terraillon, noted his skills and signed him when he was just eight years old. This allowed him to move rapidly through the youth soccer program in town. As soon as he turned 18, he was added to the Lyon first team.

His first experience with the Lyon team wasn't a pleasant one. The established team players made fun of him. This prompted him to say, "Do not laugh at me. Remember, I was once a ball boy to you all, but now, I'm here to compete, take the club's number 10 shirt, and take your places."

These were powerful words from a newcomer to the team, but they were backed up by his skills and dedication. He took the number 9 shirt, and eventually earned number 10.

His first professional appearance for Lyon was as a substitute in the Lyon-Metz match. Lyon won 2-0, with Benzema an assist for the second goal.

In his first season, he played six games and Lyon won the League title.

Unfortunately, his second season wasn't as successful. Lyon had signed Brazilian striker Fred, and he got most of the time on the field. Benzema was relegated to the substitute position. But rather than getting downhearted, Benzema focused on giving his all when he was on the field.

Showing his skill led to him playing more often, and a pattern started to develop. Although he was generally brought on as a substitute, he nearly always scored. Unfortunately, he suffered a thigh injury, which knocked him out of action for three months. Then his return from injury started a goalless streak that lasted for the rest of the season.

In the 2007-0008 season, he really started to shine. When several players left the club, Benzema was given the number 10 shirt and became the team's lead striker.

The opportunity wasn't wasted on Benzema. He scored 31 goals in 51 games and helped Lyon win their first-ever double—the Coup de la Ligue and the Coupe de France. One of his most impressive accomplishments that season was a hat trick against Metz.

In addition, his play against Manchester United in the Champions League earned Benzema praise from Sir Alex Ferguson.

Benzema signed a new contract with Lyon and started the 2008-2009 season well. This prompted the club's president to put a €100 million price tag on the star, ensuring no one would be interested in poaching him.

Unfortunately, Benzema saw a dip in his form after the winter break. Goals became sporadic, and the team lost the League title—the first they had lost in eight years.

The following season, Benzema found himself transferred to Real Madrid. Unfortunately, his sporadic form continued. While Benzema did score goals in some matches, he wasn't consistent. This prompted the manager to use him as a substitute for the second part of the season.

Like so many before him, it appeared that Benzema's career was over before he had really reached his stride. Even the local papers criticized him for underperforming and making no attempt to learn the language.

To make things worse, the 2010-2011 season saw a change in management at Real Madrid. The new manager wasn't a fan of Benzema, nor was the French national team coach. They both acknowledged that Benzema was talented, but they felt that talent alone wasn't enough. He needed to start working harder and improve his fitness.

This was a rough time for Benzema. He spent much of the season on the bench and went goalless for two months.

Eventually, Higuain, the team's main striker, was injured, giving Benzema a starting spot on the team. This gave him the chance to score. Gradually, throughout the season, he started to impress his coach. He became instrumental in Real Madrid's Copa del Rey performance, helping them to win the cup and gaining praise from his coach in the process.

This success marked a change in Benzema. Before the 2011-2012 season started, he had undergone weight loss treatment and physical training to build his muscle mass. This had made a huge difference in his stamina and ability to play.

This, and the fact he was finally integrating with the team and the culture in Spain, made all the difference. Ultimately, it was his decision to take himself and his role more seriously that led to numerous goals and his recognition as one of the greatest soccer players in the world.

By the end of 2016, Benzema had helped lead Real Madrid to 10 titles. He also started to accumulate records, such as making over 500 appearances for Real Madrid and being the club's sixth all-time goal scorer.

Over the years he has grown as a player, recording some of the best goals soccer has ever seen. In short, he's an inspiration, showing other soccer players and non-players what is possible when you try.

FUN FACTS ABOUT KARIM BENZEMA

- His transfer to Real Madrid cost $35 million—a record at the time.
- His younger brothers are also professional footballers, just not quite as well-known
- He could have played for Algeria or France: he was born in France but is of Algerian descent, making him eligible for both teams.
- He has the record for the fastest goal in La Liga—just 22 seconds!
- He's the oldest player to score a Champions League hat trick!

QUICK TRIVIA TEST

What team did Karim Benzema first play for?

AS Bron Terraillon.

Which season at Real Madrid did he spend most of the time on the bench?

His second season with them: 2006-2007.

When was Benzema born?

In 1987

What number jersey did he get at Lyon?

Nine.

Which year did he receive weight treatment?

2011.

FIVE LIFE LESSONS

1. "Even when you fail, you will be stronger than if you hadn't tried."

These are words Benzema lives by. There have been many times in his life when he has tried to do something and failed, just as there are in everyone's life.

Failure happens, but it helps you know how to do better next time. Ultimately, learning from failure leads to success.

2. Always give your best.

Benzema could have given up when he was stuck on the bench. However, he stuck to the plan, persevered, and was eventually given opportunities.

Because he tried his best, those opportunities eventually led to so much more.

3. Communication is vital

Karim Benzema said, "What I would like is to at least have a discussion with the coach, that he tells me what he thinks. I have to know".

It emphasizes the importance of communication if you want any plan to succeed.

4. Know your limits.

Benzema's teammates will tell you that his advice is often to pass the ball to him. This certainly helps the team score goals.

However, Benzema is just as good at passing as he is at receiving. He knows that no one has the right answer or position all the time. It's better to know your limits and work with those around you who can do what you can't.

5. Aim to be better.

Benzema grew up in a troubled part of France, rife with gangs. He could have easily joined one and lived that life. But his father taught him discipline and to aim higher—to be the best he could be. That's a valuable life lesson everyone should learn.

KEVIN DE BRUYNE
SURVIVING TEENAGE ANGST

Kevin De Bruyne is known as the midfielder and captain of Manchester City. He is also the star of the Belgian soccer team and is seen by many as one of the best midfielders in the world.

That's impressive, considering the competition.

De Bruyne was born in Belgium. His parents are Belgian and rather affluent. However, his mother grew up with her parents in London.

He was born in 1991, and started playing soccer in 1995, he was just four years old. His talent was immediately obvious to friends and family, who pushed the young boy to try out for the club in his hometown.

As a child, de Bruyne spent many school holidays and Christmases in the UK with family. He sees the country as a second home. As a child, he also visited Africa a lot.

In 1997, when he was just six years old, he joined KVV Drongen. De Bruyne spent two years there, working on his game. Then, when he was eight years old, he moved to Gent as part of their youth training academy.

During this period, de Bruyne honed his skills and began to show his desire to win. The young soccer player developed a reputation for causing trouble, but in reality, like many young people, he was simply frustrated when things didn't go his team's way. This was something that he learned to deal with, if he hadn't he would never have become the amazing soccer player he is today.

In 2005, at just 14, de Bruyne transferred to Genk. He was still in the youth academy, but the quality of his play had been noticed. The move was prompted by de Bruyne, as he felt the coaches were better at Genk. He was young, but he knew exactly what he wanted.

Late in 2008, he became part of the first team squad. He played his first game for the Genk first team in May of 2009. That first game was a loss, but just a couple of weeks later, he scored his first goal, securing Genk's 1-0 win against Standard Liege.

This was the first of many goals. Over the next four years, de Bruyne played for Genk 113 times. He scored 17 goals and assisted with another 36.

His hard work made a difference. Genk won the Belgian Cup in 2009, and both the Belgian Pro League and Belgian Super Cup in 2011.

During this period, his performance endeared him to the hearts of millions of Belgians and resulted in a call-up to the Belgian international team. In 2008, he played for Belgium in the under-18 side, and in 2011 he was with the under-21s.

Particularly noteworthy was his game against RSC Charleroi in August of 2010. He only played for 60 minutes of the game, yet in this time he scored two goals and assisted with another.

It was this kind of performance that built his confidence and his reputation. He quickly became known as a formidable midfielder.

Naturally, this type of talent attracted attention from the biggest clubs in the Premier League. While several clubs were interested, it was Chelsea that eventually took him for £7 million.

Interestingly, because the transfer was agreed upon mid-season, he was loaned back to Genk to finish the season. This was a rewarding experience, as de Bruyne got to play center instead of his customary left position. He performed so well that this became his position at Genk.

There was more good news for de Bruyne. Chelsea was well aware of how difficult the cultural change can be when moving to the UK. After seeing de Bruyne perform well in pre-season games, they loaned him to the Bundesliga side Werder Bremen. During his loan period, he played in 34 games, scored 10 goals, and provided 10 assists.

De Bruyne felt that he was ready to shine at Chelsea. Unfortunately, it wasn't meant to be. Despite playing well, he wasn't given much playing time. His frustration quickly boiled over, and he confronted manager Jose Mourinho.

Chelsea didn't want to loan or transfer de Bruyne, but he felt he would never get a fair chance with the team, so he pushed for a transfer. This resulted in him moving to VFL Wolfsburg in the Bundesliga. The fee was an impressive $25 million!

The club quickly saw the results of their investment. He played in 16 games in the second half of the season, scoring three goals and assisting with six more. It was enough for Wolfsburg to qualify for the Europa League.

This was a great start, but it was in the 2014-2015 season when he really showed Chelsea what they had lost out on. He scored 16 goals and assisted with 28 more in 51 games. These stats sound impressive on their own, but they don't tell you just how good his performance was. He helped the team become runner-up in the League and reach the quarterfinals of the Europa League. In short, he was consistently world-class.

Perhaps one of his greatest performances of this season was in the game against Inter Milan in the Europa League. His play enabled Wolfsburg to move on to the next stage of the competition. De Bruyne even scored twice and assisted with one goal against the Italian super team.

The next season saw de Bruyne continue his world-class performances and led to a transfer offer of £55 million from Manchester City. It was too good a deal for Wolfsburg to turn down.

His first season at Manchester City was good, despite a knee injury. But, his subsequent seasons, under new manager Pep Guardiola, have been phenomenal. Since picking up de Bruyne, Manchester City has dominated the domestic league.

He may not have felt he needed to prove himself in the Premier League, but de Bruyne has certainly made Chelsea think twice about their decision to get rid of him.

De Bruyne is also a critical element of the Belgian national team. Their rise to the top of the FIFA rankings is directly attributed to him.

FUN FACTS ABOUT KEVIN DE BRUYNE

- De Bruyne plays for Belgian, but he also could have played for Burundi. He was born in Belgium but his mother was born in Burundi, making him eligible for both teams.
- He's an avid birdwatcher!
- De Bruyne has created his own clothing and book brand.
- He was listed as the fourth-best soccer player in the world by The Guardian in 2017.
- De Bruyne was an ambassador for the 2014 Special Olympics.

QUICK TRIVIA TEST

At what age did de Bruyne start playing soccer?

Four.

Which year did he become part of the first team?

2008.

Why did he demand a transfer from Chelsea?

Not enough playing time or opportunities.

Where did de Bruyne go after Chelsea?

Wolfsburg in the Bundesliga.

Which team did he play for in the Premier League after Wolfsburg?

Manchester City.

FIVE LIFE LESSONS

1. No matter your background, it takes hard work to succeed

De Bruyne started playing soccer at a young age and had a natural talent. However, that didn't mean he was guaranteed a place as a professional soccer player.

His family background was business-related, but to get anywhere in soccer, de Bruyne needed to work hard and seize every opportunity that he received. It was this approach that proved anything was possible.

2. Stand up for yourself.

It's important to stand up for yourself and what you believe. De Bruyne did this at Chelsea when he felt he wasn't being given the opportunities he deserved.

As a result, he left Chelsea and showed his true skills at Wolfsburg.

3. Learn to deal with frustration.

As a young player, de Bruyne quickly developed a reputation for being hot-headed. He was known as a troublemaker because he would often get angry. This stemmed from frustration with his own performance.

Over the years, he has learned to deal with his frustration. This makes him a better player and a better person, both on and off the field.

4. The right team matters.

It's obvious from de Bruyne's career that the right team makes a difference. He never felt comfortable or shone at Chelsea. This was mainly because he had minimal playing time and the manager wasn't interested in giving him opportunities.

De Bruyne forced the team to transfer him, allowing him to reach his potential as a player. Of course, he could only shine with the right team around him, with everyone working together. That's important to remember.

5. Know Yourself

De Bruyne is quoted as saying "I always like to assist more than scoring: it gives me another feeling; I cannot explain it."

He's a great player and has already realized that you have to know yourself and preferences if you wish to succeed. This allows you to play to your strengths.

VINICIUS JUNIOR FROM THE STREETS TO CONQUERING THE WORLD

According to The Guardian, Vinicius Junior is the eighth-best soccer player in the world. He's currently a vital part of Real Madrid's attack team and has scored numerous times for the team.

But his path to success hasn't been guaranteed or smooth.

Vinicius Junior was born in July of 2000. His full name is Vinícius José Paixão de Oliveira Júnior, and, like so many soccer players, his childhood was marked by poverty.

He was born in Sao Goncalo, where he kicked a ball around on the streets. Although he appeared to have natural talent, his main interest was futsal, which is a game based on soccer that uses a smaller field and is played on a hard surface.

He joined the Flamengo training academy when he was just six years old, and instantly got people's attention. There was no doubt he had skills. He could play and outmatch players two or three years older than him.

However, despite his skill, when he tried out for the youth side at age nine, he was rejected. The good news was that he was advised to try again the following year. He did so and started training at the Flamengo training facility when he was 10.

His father had to get an extra job to support the family, and his mother traveled with him 70km every time he trained.

Vinicius Junior was small for his age. When he first went out onto the field in his debut match against Atletico Mineiro, he looked like a ball boy. Nonetheless, his skills did the talking for him.

That was common for the young Vinicius Junior, who was painfully shy but came alive on the field.

Junior finished the Under-17 South American Championship as the top scorer and best player. This convinced Real Madrid to sign him.

It's impressive to be signed by Real Madrid in this way, but it also means a lot of pressure to perform, especially when you are being lined up to replace the great Cristiano Ronaldo (who was leaving Real Madrid for Juventus).

Junior was described as bringing an electricity and sharpness to the team, something that was previously missing. He scored four goals and assisted with eight more out of 31 appearances. This was a credible start, perfectly showcasing his talent.

Junior also had to deal with animosity from other players. No one knows where it came from, but Karim Benzema was caught on camera saying that Junior was playing against the team. He told his teammate Mendy not to pass to Vinicius.

Junior didn't let it bother him. Instead, he maximized every opportunity he had and put the ball where it needed to be. The result was a victory for Real Madrid in the Champions League.

By the end of the season, Junior had 22 goals and 16 assists. He played in 52 games.

Junior has also had to deal with racism in the sport. One notable incident occurred when Spanish soccer agent Pedro Bravio stated that Junior's celebratory dance was "acting the monkey." He later apologized and stated he had used the phrase metaphorically.

Unfortunately, this triggered a string of racist abuse from Atletico fans when Atletico played Real Madrid. It was so bad that the Spanish Prime Minister made a statement and La Liga had to file an official report to the state's anti-violence commission.

Junior showed his maturity in this game by rising above the taunts and giving one of the best performances of his life.

Although he may have encountered issues with Spanish supporters and even the Spanish culture, he's never had an issue with the Brazilian international team.

He was first called up to the under-15 Brazilian squad in 2015. He helped Brazil to win the South American Championship and was the second top goal scorer.

The following year, he played in a friendly for Brazil under-17s. They won 4-2, with Vinicius providing two of the goals and assisting with the other two.

He continued to play for the U-17s and helped Brazil to a place in the FIFA U-17 World Cup. Brazil finished third, and Junior was named the top player of the tournament. He was also the top goal scorer.

He subsequently joined the Brazilian national team for the first time in February 2019. Unfortunately, an injury while playing for Real Madrid put him out for several international games.

He finally debuted for the Brazilian senior team in September 2019. However, he didn't manage to score a goal for the Brazilian team until 2022, when playing Chile in the FIFA World Cup qualifier.

It's worth noting that the racist incident brought support from many players around the globe, including Junior's idol Neymar, as well as Pele, Ronaldo, and Richarlison.

Off the field, Junior has started an institute in his native city of Rio that aims to give more children access to education and sport.

When it comes to soccer, Junior has continued to do what he does best, answer the negative comments by playing even better on the field. He has continued to showcase his talent throughout the 2023 season, there is clearly more to come from the Brazilian superstar.

FUN FACTS ABOUT VINICIUS JUNIOR

- Real Madrid paid £38.7 million for Junior, a record for someone under age 19.
- Vinicius Junior is a huge basketball fan.
- He's the first player born in 2000 or later to play for Real Madrid.
- Vinicius Junior nearly pursued futsal instead of soccer.
- He was initially rejected by the Flamengo training facility.

QUICK TRIVIA TEST

What is Vinicius Junior's full name?

Vinícius José Paixão de Oliveira Júnior.

Who is Vinicius Junior's idol?

Neymar, who recently described Vinicius as the best in the world!

Who replaced Junior on the Brazilian squad after his Real Madrid injury?

David Neres.

What age was he when he first played for Brazil?

15.

What career path did Vinicius Junior nearly follow instead of soccer?

Futsal.

FIVE LIFE LESSONS

1. Rise to any occasion.

Vinicius Junior could have buckled under the pressure of replacing Cristiano Ronaldo. Instead, he rose to the occasion and brought a new sense of purpose to the Spanish side.

This earned him high praise, especially when it was said he had a bit of both Ronaldos in him.

2. Rise above other people's issues.

Junior faced a real challenge on the field when he was subjected to vile racist abuse by the Atletico fans. He could have let it get to him and ruin his performance.

Instead, he chose to rise above their petty taunts and let his soccer do the talking.

It's important to know when to stand and argue, and when to simply let your actions speak louder than words.

3. Focus on your goal.

Moving from Brazil to Europe wasn't easy. Junior was young and had to integrate with a new team, replace an international superstar, and deal with a different culture.

He managed all this by staying focused on his goal—to play soccer to the best of his ability.

4. Perseverance matters.

Vinicius Junior looks and acts like a soccer star. He remains calm under pressure and has a collection of trophies to confirm his talent.

This hasn't always been the case. He's had to work hard and persevere through injuries and being overlooked. This has helped define his character and make him the player he is today.

5. Be true to yourself.

This is perhaps the biggest lesson that anyone can learn, and applies to all walks of life. Being true to yourself means you can sleep soundly at night.

Vinicius Junior demonstrated this perfectly when he refused to keep quiet after the racist attacks. He even called out the president of La Liga for his conduct, even though that could have backfired and caused problems for him.

ZINEDINE ZIDANE
LEGENDARY PLAYER & COACH

Mention Zinedine Zidane today, and most people will instantly think of his coaching success.

Perhaps most notable was his coaching of Real Madrid. Although he originally resisted the idea of coaching, a direct appeal from José Mourinho led to an advisory position in 2010. By 2011, he was the sporting director for the club. In 2013, he became the assistant coach. The following year, he became the Real Madrid B team coach. He was effectively in charge of the first team, as well. Finally, his position as head coach was confirmed in 2016.

His official coaching career had a great start, with Real Madrid winning their first League game 5-0. Shortly after that, Real Madrid beat Barcelona for the first time in 39 games.

Just a few months later, Zidane led the team to the Champions League European Cup final, where they won the championship via a penalty shootout. This was the 11th time Real Madrid had won it. With that win, Zidane became only the seventh player to win the championship as both a player and a coach.

Real Madrid also ended up second in the League, just one point behind Barcelona—not bad for a first season as an official coach!

The following season was possibly even better, as the club set a new record. They played 35 matches without losing a single one. By the end of 2016, Real Madrid had the FIFA Club World Cup trophy to add to their collection.

That second season, Zidane once again led the team in winning the La Liga. It was the 33rd time the club had won the league, but the first time in five years.

While Zidane has an enviable record as the coach of Real Madrid, he's much more than that. He's also one of the greatest soccer players to ever live.

Zidane was born in 1972 in Marseille, France. Both his parents were of Algerian descent. Although they were hard-working, they lived in a crime-ridden housing development known as La Castellane.

Money was tight, and their house wasn't big enough for all seven members of the family to sit together and eat. This is reportedly what inspired Zidane to lift his family out of poverty.

Even as a child, Zidane had natural talent and knew this was a way to help his family financially.

His talent was quickly noticed, and he joined the Saint-Henri soccer club in 1981, when he was just nine years old. In those early days, he was constantly exposed to racial slurs and teased about his poor background.

Zidane used this aggression against him as motivation and channeled his anger into his game. His impressive performances resulted in an option to transfer to Septèmes-les-Vallons. He seized this opportunity and stayed there until 1986, honing his skills.

He then spent three years at US Saint-Henri before transferring to Cannes in 1989.

After three years on the Cannes youth team, he joined the senior squad. But he immediately got into trouble and almost ruined his promising career before it even started. The racial slurs had continued, and this time Zidane decided to fight back, punching another player. This led to him spending most of his senior career on the bench, assigned cleaning duties.

Despite this, his skills on the field helped Cannes finish fourth in the league. It was the club's highest finish since 1949!

In 1992, Zidane managed to secure a transfer to Bordeaux, where he really started to shine. His midfield combinations with Bixente Lizarazu and Christophe Dugarry became the trademark plays of Bordeaux and the French squad.

1996 was perhaps his greatest club year. Zidane played so well that he was offered contracts with a variety of top European clubs. Instead, he chose to move to Juventus. While there, he was noted as being a selfless player. In every game, his sole aim was to help the team.

1998 was both a good and bad year for Zidane. He won the FIFA World Player of the Year and the Ballon d'Or, but he was also banned after head-butting Jochen Kientz in the group stages of the Champions League.

Although his image was tainted, the clubs could still see his talent, and he moved to Real Madrid in 2001. This was where he scored perhaps his most famous goal. A high pass came directly to Zidane, and in one movement he managed to leap, turn, and catch the volley full force with his left foot. It shot past the defenders and the keeper, and into the back of the net. The fact that it was the winning goal of the Champions League final was the icing on the cake. Zidane's reaction was perfect as he ran toward the goal, his mouth wide open, screaming in delight.

Zidane is also noted for his performances for France on the international stage. He was part of the Euro 1996 squad and was also selected to play for France in the 1998 World Cup, here he was instrumental with his goal assists. The team made it to the final, where Zidane scored two of the three winning goals. It was the first time France had won the World Cup!

This made Zidane a national hero—a status that was reinforced when France won Euro 2000, becoming the first team, since West Germany in 1974, to have the World Cup and European Championship at the same time.

France struggled in future tournaments but did well in the 2006 World Cup when Zidane came out of retirement. He helped them reach the final and gave them an early lead.

Thanks to his impressive career, his never say die attitude, and his efforts and achievements as a coach, the name Zidane is now famous for being one of the best players and coaches the soccer world has ever seen.

FUN FACTS ABOUT ZINEDINE ZIDANE

- He was Qatar's ambassador, successfully lobbying for them to host the 2022 World Cup.
- Zidane is one of only nine players to have won the Ballon d'Or, the Champions League, and the World Cup.
- He met his wife when he was just 17.
- Zidane has the record (tied with Brazil's Cafu) for the most red cards in World Cup matches.
- He had a red card in his last game, but as he was no longer playing he couldn't serve a match ban. Instead, he was required to do community service.

QUICK TRIVIA TEST

When was Zidane born?

1972.

What year did he transfer to Bordeaux?

1992.

Which cup did Real Madrid win for the first time in five years after Zidane started officially coaching them?

European Cup.

Which World Cup did Zidane help France to win?

1998.

How many times was Zidane sent off in his career?

14!

FIVE LIFE LESSONS

1. Anger doesn't get you anywhere.

Zidane is the perfect example of why giving in to anger doesn't help. He's been banned multiple times for reacting out of anger on the field. Even in his last game, he was given a red card for punching another player.

This was a sad way for one of the greatest players to end his soccer career. Today, he has learned to control anger and is known as one of the calmest men in the sport!

This is something he tries to instill in his players.

2. Never give up.

Zidane was a national hero, but his reputation was seriously damaged by the World Cup headbutting incident.

He could have retreated, staying out of soccer and enjoying his money. Instead, he remained invested in the game. He now has an enviable reputation as both a player and a coach.

3. Never look back

Zidane believes that you can learn from your mistakes but shouldn't dwell on them. This allows you to use the knowledge to improve your life and decisions in the future.

As he says: "Life is full of regrets, but it doesn't pay to look back."

4. Downtime is important.

Playing and coaching soccer are both extremely stressful jobs. It's essential that you have a way to de-stress and retain balance in life. This is true in all walks of life. After all, excessive stress can be a killer.

Zidane makes sure he plays other sports, reads books, and spends quality time with his family. He's found that these are the best ways to de-stress.

You can choose to de-stress in whatever way is best for you—just make sure you choose something.

5. Do it for the right reasons.

Zidane grew up in a very small house, with very little money—and his family wasn't even the worst off in the area.

As a youngster, the need to get his family out of poverty was his driving force. Today, his family helps to manage him professionally, and he takes good care of them.

Zidane attributes part of his success to having the right motivation to succeed.

SAM KERR
PLAYING IN A MALE
DOMINATED SPORT

Sam Kerr was born in Australia in September 1993. She's an example of what is possible, even in a sport previously dominated by men.

Kerr currently plays for Chelsea in the FA Women's Super League. She's also the captain of the Australian women's national soccer team.

Her speed, determination, and skills have made her one of the most in-demand female strikers in the world. Many consider her to be one of the best strikers on the planet!

Kerr has won the Golden Boot in three different leagues and is the only female soccer player to have achieved this. However, while she may enjoy legendary status today, it's been a long and challenging road to get here.

Born Samantha May Kerr, she has two brothers and one sister. Her father played Australian rules soccer, which is a contact version of soccer where handballing is allowed (although you can't run with the ball). To score, the ball must go through the goalposts without being touched by another player.

Her brother also started to play Australian rules soccer, and she joined in.

This is an intense sport, and the young girl found herself getting injured too often. Although she wasn't a fan of soccer, she decided to switch sports. She was 12 at the time.

Naturally, she encountered a few difficulties switching between sports. After all, the rules are different!

Fortunately, she was naturally gifted. After three years of hard work learning the game, she was spotted by a scout from Perth Glory. At 15, she was offered a spot on the team and took it.

In 2009, she debuted in the W-League. That is when she started taking soccer seriously.

The 2009 W-League Awards saw her receive a Goal of the Year award for her outstanding goal against Sydney FC. She grabbed the ball just inside Sydney's half, gracefully moved around several players, and launched a shot at the goal from 35 yards out. The ball went straight into the top corner, and the shot drew comparisons to the great Maradona.

The following season, she started in all 10 matches and scored three goals.

In 2011, she scored her first brace and began drawing attention from outside Australia. Then, in 2013, she accepted a transfer to Western New York Flash, a well-established team in the United Women's Soccer League in the US.

After two years with the Flash, she returned to Perth Glory for a season. She played in the second match, against Adelaide United, and scored, helping Perth to victory. She scored again in the next match but was then forced to sit four matches out due to injury.

Kerr recovered and finished the season for Perth strong, scoring eight goals in just four games. Unfortunately, in early 2015 her goal against Melbourne Victory was the only one she scored. An ankle injury prevented her from playing the rest of the season.

Between 2015 and 2017, Kerr also played for Sky Blue FC. She was chosen after her performance in the FIFA Women's World Cup, which had been held in Canada. Her 2015 appearances were limited due to training with the Australian squad for the Rio Olympics. However, in 2016, she scored five goals in nine appearances. She was named NWSL Player of the Week after her impressive goals against Orlando Pride.

The following season, she played even better Kerr scored 17 goals during the season, setting a new record. She even scored four goals in one game and made the top of the NWSL scoring table.

The following season, she was traded to the Chicago Red Stars. She struggled to adjust to the new team, and it took her eight games to rediscover her form. However, for the rest of the season, she was on fire, scoring 18 goals in total and winning her second Golden Boot.

Perth extended her contract, and she returned the following season. It had been a tough battle back to full fitness, but the effort was worth it. Kerr scored 10 goals in the 2016-2017 W-League—enough to take Perth to the Grand Final.

Her efforts were rewarded with the Julie Dolan Medal and the Penny Tanner Media MVP Award

By 2018, Kerr was once again being scouted from overseas. She was offered a $300,000 contract, but Perth didn't want to lose her and offered her $400,000. In the end, she took Perth's offer, choosing to stay in her home nation.

In recognition of her excellence, she was named Player of the Year by the National Women's Soccer League Player Association!

This opened the door to Kerr's world domination. Top clubs in England were taking notice, and Chelsea swooped in, giving her a

2.5-year contract starting in January 2020. She scored just two weeks after starting and helped Chelsea win the League Cup Final. They also won the League, despite COVID-19 restrictions.

Her form has continued, with a hat trick against Bristol City while defending Chelsea's League title, and her second Women's Super League title. In the 2020-2021 season, she scored 21 goals and won another Golden Boot.

Chelsea extended her contract, and Kerr has continued to be a stunning player, goal-maker, and scorer.

Of course, her excellence hasn't just been limited to Chelsea. At 15 years of age, she helped Australia's senior team win the AFC Women's Asia Cup in 2010 and the 2011 FIFA Women's World Cup. She was also critical to Australia's second-place finish in the 2015 FIFA Women's World Cup.

In 2017, Kerr helped Australia win the inaugural Tournament of Nations and get to the knockout stage of the 2019 FIFA Women's World Cup. Australia also won bronze at the 2020 Tokyo Olympics. In addition, despite missing the first three games due to injury, Kerr helped Australia reach the semifinals in the World Cup.

All of this is pretty impressive for a player who only got serious about soccer when she was 18! And Kerr hasn't hit her peak yet, so the best is likely still to come!

FUN FACTS ABOUT SAM KERR

- Kerr is the leading Australian scorer. She's scored 42 goals in 88 international matches.
- She's won the PFA Women's Scorer of the Year Award four times!
- She was the second Australian female soccer player to receive a Medal of the Order of Australia.
- Kerr was the first Australian soccer player to score a hat trick at a World Cup tournament.
- Perth Glory Striker said her athleticism and raw talent were exceptional. She was just 13 at the time!

QUICK TRIVIA TEST

What's Kerr's full name?

Samantha May Kerr.

What sport did her father play?

Australian rules soccer.

What age was she when she debuted for Perth Glory?

15

Which team was she playing when she earned her Goal of the Year award?

Sydney FC.

How much did Perth offer Kerr to stay with them?

$400,000.

FIVE LIFE LESSONS

1. Never quit.

Kerr suffered a variety of injuries playing Australian rules soccer, and she suffered even more when she started to play soccer.

Any of those injuries could have put her out of the game for good. However, she was determined to make her mark and continue doing something she loved.

After each injury, she fought her way back to full fitness and improved her on-field performance. In short, she never quit.

2. Believe in yourself.

Sam Kerr has been quoted as saying "Winning starts with self-belief." It's something she believes has helped her achieve her potential and become the success she is today.

It's also something that anyone can do, believing in yourself is the first step to making your dreams come true.

3. Be open to anything.

As a youngster, Kerr was passionate about Australian rules soccer. She was also good at it. However, too many injuries made her think twice about the sport.

That's when she switched to soccer, even though she wasn't super keen on it. This was an unexpected change that worked out well.

4. Embrace pressure.

Not everyone likes to work under pressure—but some people do. Kerr has admitted she thrives under pressure, knowing that one moment can transform a game.

Even if you're not a fan of pressure, you can use it to motivate you and bring out the best in your performance, as Kerr does.

5. Think big.

Kerr has become one of the biggest female soccer stars in the world. However, she likes to think bigger. In recent years, she has focused on off-field leadership and how you can achieve things for the larger community when you work together.

She thinks big and thinks of others. That's something we should all try to do.

BONUS MATERIAL: INSPIRATIONAL SOCCER STORIES

100 Affirmation To Inspire And Boost Your Self-Confidence

Affirmations are best described as positive statements about yourself. Repeating all or some of them daily will encourage you to believe what you're saying. This will help you to create a positive mental outlet and believe in yourself.

1. My opinions are important
2. I am worth listening to
3. I am mentally strong
4. I have feelings that matter
5. I'm a good person
6. Anything is possible if you try hard enough
7. A positive mindset can help you achieve the impossible
8. I face one fear every day
9. I am who I am and that's a good thing
10. I love myself
11. I'm worthy of respect
12. I'm a good soccer player
13. I can learn anything
14. I'm prepared to stand up for what I believe in
15. Everyone makes mistakes, I learn from mine
16. I can overcome any obstacle
17. I make good decisions
18. I trust myself
19. I am confident
20. I am good at solving problems
21. I'm a natural leader
22. I don't follow others blindly but choose my own path

23. I will succeed
24. I trust my own instincts
25. I focus on learning something new daily
26. I see the positive in everyone and everything
27. I always look for the joy in life
28. Everyone has a good side
29. Opportunities are everywhere, and I'm ready to seize them
30. Every morning I look in the mirror and smile
31. I'm a great listener
32. I'm curious about everything, and that's a good thing
33. I try to make someone smile every day
34. I'm good at helping others
35. I'm patient with others
36. I'm kind to others
37. Embracing change is a good thing
38. I don't need to fill the silence with noise
39. I always pause to consider my actions before acting
40. I take time to exercise daily
41. Practicing soccer daily is important to me
42. I am ready and able to learn something new
43. I will persevere, no matter what the obstacles are
44. I make friends easily
45. I appreciate criticism as a chance to grow mentally and physically
46. Putting my friends first is important to me
47. Everyone is worthy in their way
48. Other people usually like me straight away
49. I'm happy to share with others
50. I play well in a team
51. I'm proud to be part of a team
52. I'm flexible and adaptable
53. I listen to my elders, managers, elders, and coaches, they generally know what they are talking about
54. Honesty really is the best policy

55. Miracles do happen
56. I know how to share my emotions and plans
57. I choose my own boundaries
58. I ask for help when I need to
59. I appreciate the importance of rest and recovery
60. I choose to eat healthily
61. It takes 5 seconds of courage to achieve anything new
62. Everyone is beautiful
63. I'm beautiful inside and out
64. I can tell when people are being treated unfairly
65. I set myself goals every day and achieve them
66. I can build new habits when I want
67. I behave to others how I expect them to behave toward me
68. I understand the importance of rest for physical and mental health
69. I don't need other people to justify my existence
70. I live in the present but learn from the past
71. I can cheer myself on when needed
72. Looking after my body is important
73. My body is perfect the way it is
74. I try to expand my comfort zone daily
75. I can forgive anyone who asks
76. I'm not afraid to apologize when I make a mistake
77. I'm entitled to my own opinion and respect other opinions
78. Any day can become a good day
79. I can change anything
80. Failure is simply an opportunity to improve
81. I love myself even when I fail
82. Finding balance in life is important to me
83. I am intelligent
84. I can do it!
85. I am always a good friend
86. I set a good example for others
87. Money isn't the most important thing in life

88. I choose to be happy
89. I stand up for those in need
90. I prefer to say nice things about people
91. I accept everyone just the way they are
92. I get better every day
93. My positive energy helps others
94. My actions make a difference
95. I love learning new things
96. I take care of my possessions
97. I'm here to support loved ones whenever they need it
98. I embrace my emotions because my feelings are valid
99. I know my problems don't define me, it's how I react that matters
100. I am always in control of myself

Developing A Positive Mental Mindset

Soccer is more than a way to stay fit or make friends, it can be a lifelong commitment and a potentially lucrative career. However, to make the most of the opportunity you need to start with a positive mental mindset. You're never too young to start developing this.

Learn to Lose

Most people play sports, including soccer, to win. However, it's virtually impossible to win every game or even every tackle. You can get upset and angry when you lose, but this won't help you mentally prepare for future games.

Instead, you need to learn that losing happens. When it does, focus on the good things in the game and consider what went wrong. It will make you better at accepting loss, and a more graceful winner.

Try Again And Again

Persistence is one of the most important mental qualities all soccer players need. You'll often need stamina and persistence just to finish the game. It's important to think about persistence before you even step onto the field.

Remind yourself that you're committed to the game and your team, you need to finish what you start. The best way to build this mindset is to set yourself goals every day, and make them achievable but not too easy. That way you'll try, fail, and try again. After all, the feeling of success is amazing.

Failure Is A Growth Opportunity

Failure happens and while trying again will help you to build perseverance, it will also help you learn and improve. Every failure, whether it's a lost game, missed goal, or even running late for training, gives you an opportunity to reflect on what went wrong and how to do better next time.

Create Your Own Motto

A positive mental attitude is a deliberate choice. You can choose to dwell on what has gone wrong or decide to focus on how you can make it happen. The second choice gives you a positive mindset. To develop this you need to create your own motto, it can even be one of the affirmations in this book. Repeat your chosen affirmations and your motto daily and you'll develop a positive mindset, making you ready for anything the beautiful game has to offer.

Accept Criticism

There will always be those who criticize you just for the sake of it. However, when those you love and trust offer you criticism you should accept it. They are telling you what they perceive to be the problem. In many cases, they can see things you can't because they have a different perspective. Listen to the criticism and use it to become a better player.

Developing a positive mindset takes time. However, it starts with a simple step, choosing to adopt a positive approach. The rest just takes perseverance.

A Young Person's Guide To Playing Soccer

The basic aim of any soccer game is to score more goals than the opposing team. Before you can start playing you need to have the right equipment and a good understanding of the rules. The following will help!

Equipment

Soccer is played on a grass field which is a minimum of 10 yards long and 70 yards wide. Most teams play on a field 115 yards long and 75 yards wide. The edge of the field is marked with white lines and there is one goal at each end.

Players will usually wear shin pads to protect their legs when accidentally kicked. The keeper will also have a set of gloves as they are the only players allowed to touch the ball with their hands. All players will wear soccer boots, these have studs on to help players grip on grass. They aren't necessary for artificial surfaces.

Rules of the game

Every game lasts 90 minutes, it's split into two halves of 45 minutes each. During that time, the ball must completely cross the goal line for a goal to count. If anything happens during the game that stops play, the referee tracks the amount of time the game has been stopped for and adds it to the end of the game. It's referred to as stoppage time.

In tournaments, when a clear winner is necessary, if the score is still zero-zero at the end of stoppage time there will be 30 minutes of extra time. If that doesn't resolve the game then each side will take penalties to find a winner.

Each time must have at least seven players and a maximum of 11. Of course, teams are usually 11 players. The ball must stay on the field between the designated lines. If it goes past the lines the team which didn't touch it last gets to throw the ball in from the side, or kick it in from the corner.

Heading is allowed, as is kicking, but your hands are not allowed to touch the ball unless you're a goalie. Dangerous, reckless, or play using excessive force will be classed as an offense. The referee can issue a warning, a yellow card, or a red card. Getting a red card means you have to leave the field and your team carries on a player down. Offenses give the opposite team a free kick.

It's worth noting that youth soccer is played on a slightly smaller field. It's common to only have seven players.

Positions

There are four main positions in the game of soccer:

Forwards

Forwards are the players who create spaces for goals and ultimately score them. You need to be good at controlling the ball and shooting at a target. Dribbling skills are often considered essential to get you around the opposing team players. Forwards frequently pass the ball back and forth between them to move it forward and secure a shooting opportunity.

To be a successful forward you need to be good at finding space and always be aware of where the other players are. This increases the chances of your team scoring.

Midfield

The midfield is situated between the defense and the forwards. Their job is to connect the two. In other words, as the defense clears the ball from the goal area, the midfielder will receive it and pass it forward to the forwards. These are the players who get the attack rolling, allowing the forwards to finish the job.

Midfielders need to have plenty of stamina and a high level of fitness. They will run back and forth on the field, often more than any other player. They don't need to be able to shoot, although that can occasionally be useful. However, they do need to be accurate at passing.

Defense

Defenders sit between the opposing team and the goal. Their job is to, keep the ball away from their own goal. Defenders need to be confident on the field and ready to tackle anyone. It's important they are aware of where all the players are, this will allow them to tackle an opponent and then pass the ball to the midfield, or even another defender if necessary.

Defenders are the players most likely to be called to cover a different position if the team needs them to do so.

Goalkeeper

The goalkeeper is the last person between the opposing team's forwards and a goal. They have to be capable of reading other players and identifying where they are likely to shoot. They can then dive across the goal to catch the ball.

They need to have fantastic reflexes and be highly accurate when throwing or kicking the ball forward to their teammates.

The Offside Rule

A foul or other offense stops play and the other side gets a free kick. Equally, the ball going out of the field stops play and the opposing side gets possession. Provided you use your feet and don't use excessive force, the ball effectively stays in play. However, players need to be aware of the offside rule, this will stop play and pass the ball to the opposition.

Any player who is nearer the opponent's goal than the ball and the second-to-last player is considered offside, but only if they connect with the ball. In other words, when receiving the ball, make sure there is at least one defender and a goalkeeper between you and the goal.

To get started in soccer you'll want to practice shooting at a goal. You should be able to get it on target every time. In addition, you should work on your general fitness. It can be exhausting running up and down a field for 90 minutes. You'll also want to learn good ball control skills. That's keeping the ball at your feet while running and moving around obstacles. You can practice this in your yard. At the same time, you should be aware of where the other players are, allowing you to pass, dribble, or even tackle as necessary.

With that in mind, all you need to do is practice.

Made in the USA
Columbia, SC
30 October 2024

45258637R00076